# EVERYTHING

*is*

# NEGOTIABLE

# EVERYTHING

*is*

# NEGOTIABLE

Achieving Your True Worth by Successfully Negotiating

## Robert T. Uda

Internationally Recognized, Award-Winning Author

iUniverse, Inc.
New York  Lincoln  Shanghai

**Everything is Negotiable**
**Achieving Your True Worth by Successfully Negotiating**

iUniverse books may be ordered through booksellers or by contacting:

iUniverse
2021 Pine Lake Road, Suite 100
Lincoln, NE 68512
www.iuniverse.com
1-800-Authors (1-800-288-4677)


ISBN-13: 978-0-595-40729-3 (pbk)
ISBN-13: 978-0-595-85094-5 (ebk)
ISBN-10: 0-595-40729-3 (pbk)
ISBN-10: 0-595-85094-4 (ebk)

Printed in the United States of America

*Everything is Negotiable* is dedicated to all job seekers who know exactly what they are worth and who will accept only salary offers with which they are totally satisfied.

# Contents

# Preface

*Everything is Negotiable* provides you with strategies and tactics that you can apply in a job search to maximize your salary negotiating abilities and leave nothing on the table. It includes principles, secrets, and ideas for negotiating the salary figure you want and getting paid for what you are really worth. *Everything is Negotiable* will open eyes, cause outside-of-the-box thinking, and promulgate paradigm shifts.

*Everything is Negotiable: Achieving Your True Worth by Successfully Negotiating* works hand-in-hand with five of my other related books. They are as follows:

- *Career Quest for Young Professionals: How to Maintain a Competitive Edge Over Your Peers*
- *Career Quest for College Graduates: Developing a Successful Career by Leveraging Each of Your Jobs*
- *Career Quest for College Students: Career Development for Those Who Plan to Have a Successful Career*
- *Resumes That Pack a Punch! Creating Beefy Bullets That Grab, Hook, and Wow Hiring Managers into Calling You for an Interview*
- *What Hue Is Your Bungee Cord? Job Searching Strategies for Those Over 40 Years of Age*

If you learn, internalize, and apply the principles within this book, you will seal a salary offer that represents exactly what you are worth.

If you disagree with anything that I have written in this book, I encourage you to write me and voice your disagreement. I always like to hear and learn about other people's views on whatever I write. Never do I believe that I know all truth on anything. I am always willing to change my views if someone comes up with contrary responses that make sense to me. That being said, I look forward to hearing from you.

All writings and opinions in this book are solely mine. Any error would be my error only. If you find errors, please bring them to my attention. We will correct them in subsequent editions of this book. I hope you enjoy the real-life stories in this book as I thoroughly have enjoyed living and writing about them. Thank you.

Robert T. Uda
San Marcos, California
November 2006

*Chapter 1*

# Everything is Negotiable!

---

*If you assume everything is negotiable, you'll find that it's true. Ordinarily, a situation doesn't preclude you from negotiating. Instead, it dictates how you need to go about trying to get what you want. Successful women recognize that almost everything is negotiable, although you don't want to negotiate everything. You decide what's worth negotiating.*[1]

> Lee E. Miller, managing director of NegotiationPlus.com,
> and Jessica Miller, commercial real-estate executive

## Fallacy—"You cannot get good offers in today's job environment."

This belief is a bunch of malarkey. You can receive good job offers in any job market. If it is a job seeker's market, you can obtain good job offers. If it is a hiring company's market, you can still get good job offers. It is a matter of belief and perception. If you believe you can acquire good job offers, you will. If the hiring manager perceives you to be a good catch, he/she will give you a good job offer.

> *They always allow for negotiating room.*

Hence, don't ever take the first offer...negotiate it up! No hiring authority in his/her right mind ever makes an initial offer as a best-and-final offer (BAFO). *They always allow for negotiating room.* However, many job seekers are so desperate and fearful of the company withdrawing the offer that they cower and quickly accept the initial offer. That's foolishness!

---

1   Lee E. Miller and Jessica Miller, "Four Negotiation Tips for Women Executives," CareerJournal.com, The Wall Street Journal Executive Career Site, August 5, 2003.

## You Are Worth Only What You Accept

### Leave Nothing On the Table

In many cases, they leave thousands of dollars on the negotiating table. Remember, *you are worth only what you accept.* If you accept the $90K per year initial offer instead of negotiating it up to the negotiating maximum leeway the hiring authority has (let's say $105K), then you leave $15K on the negotiating table, and all you're really worth is $90K, not $105K. The hiring authority thought you were worth $105K, but you proved him/her otherwise.

> *You are worth only what you accept.*

### Don't Accept Offers Too Quickly

This also can backfire on a candidate. If you accept the offer too quickly, they might feel you are more desperate than they first realized. Further, you might induce "second thoughts" in the hiring manager. More important, you are not appreciated for your negotiating ability and strengths.

### Negotiating Finesse and Balance

There is a balance here as well. If you push too hard, they might ignore your counter and perceive you as greedy or self-serving. Thus, negotiating forcefully works against you. You must walk a tight wire. It is all about negotiating finesse and balance.

> *Once a company decides to hire you, it would take a lot for them to retract their offer.*

## You Have Maximum Leverage Power

*Once a company decides to hire you, it would take a lot for them to retract their offer.* After they invest a lot of time, energy, and money finding you, interviewing you, flying you in for an on-site interview, and wooing you, they are committed to the pending relationship. At this point, you have maximum leverage power. You should take advantage of this leverage by actively negotiating better terms of the offer.

## Ask and You Shall Receive

Neither be demanding nor sound too anxious, pushy, or desperate. All you should do is to *suggest, ask,* or *request* their consideration on the additional pay, incentives, benefits, and perks you desire. You would be amazed how much a company will throw at you just for the asking. *Ask and you shall receive.*

> **Ask and you shall receive.**

### Be Ready with a Good Explanation

However, when asking for additional pay, incentives, benefits, and perks, provide an explanation as to why you are asking for such additional consideration. Often, if a plausible explanation is offered, the company will not think you are being greedy or attempting to exploit the process and the company.

### Prepare a Comparison Matrix

Here is what I did. I prepared a matrix comparing the offers of my last three jobs plus the three offers I received during this recent job search. This comparison matrix, along with justification text in a cover letter for each of the six negotiating points that I had asked for, constituted my initial negotiating position. I received concurrence of three of the six negotiating points plus an additional desktop computer in my home (that I hadn't asked for). I was happy with the outcome of the negotiations and accepted the offer.

> **Hiring companies always have wiggle room.**

### *They Always Have Wiggle Room*

Remember, *hiring companies **always** have wiggle room*. In most cases, they will increase base salary and relocation allowance. If they cannot increase the base salary, they may throw a sign-on bonus at you, increase your stock options, give you a lucrative incentive/performance bonus plan, and/or throw a whole bunch of perks at you.

### *Always Negotiate a Better Offer*

Yes, in today's job environment, it may be a hiring companies market rather than a job seekers market. However, that does not mean you cannot maximize what you deserve. Remember, they are hiring you for your skills to solve their problems. If you refuse to negotiate, then shame on you.

### Negotiating Points

In this current environment, to increase the original offer, negotiating results that you can seek include the following:

- Salary increase
- Basic relocation allowance (moving costs, house-hunting trips, temporary housing, and per diem)
- Incentive bonus plan
- Temporary housing (amount or length of time)
- Travel allowance (amount or length of time)
- Full cost of cell phone including cost of all calls
- Payment of annual dues for membership in professional societies
- Vacation time
- Education reimbursement
- Laptop computer or additional desktop in your home

*You can ask for just about anything—whatever the market will bear.* When the job seeker's market returns in the future, other negotiating results that you can ask for include the following:

> *You can ask for just about anything— whatever the market will bear.*

- Stock options
- Sign-on bonus
- Relocation expenses such as payment of real estate fees and closing costs including gross-up on taxes (this is in addition to the basic relocation package)
- Purchase of your home (and the company resells it)
- Leased automobile
- Company charge card

## Take All the Time You Need

*Never rush the negotiations.* Take as much time as you and the company need. Never act scared or hard up. Negotiate your job offer the way you would negotiate a contract for the company if you went to work for them. How you negotiate your job offer with the company gives the hiring manager a clue on how you would negotiate contracts for them.

> **Never rush the negotiations.**

## Mutually Beneficial Relationship

Do not act like they are doing you a favor by hiring you. You are doing them a favor by going to work for them because they are hiring you to solve their problems. If you are going to work for them just for the pay that you will be receiving, you are accepting the job for the wrong reason. *Be humble, but move with confidence, determination, and respect.* Both parties should benefit mutually and equally from the pending employment relationship.

> **Be humble, but move with confidence, determination, and respect.**

## Reject Cheapskate Companies

### A Matter of Perspective

If a company will not negotiate with you, then you shouldn't go to work for them. After you go to work for them, they are going to be miserly and chintzy on everything. You don't want to work for such companies. There are many good companies for which to work. When the market turns back to a job seeker's market, hiring companies will start throwing money, bonuses, benefits, stock options, and perks at you just to outdo their competitors. It is all a matter of perspective.

### Reject Companies That Only Want Indentured Servants

I rejected one cheapskate company that would not give me a bonus plan. They wanted me to prepare winning proposals to capture millions and millions of dollars of new business for them, but all they wanted to give me was a salary, which was about 15 percent below what I was previously making! What a bunch of cheapskates! All they were looking for was an indentured servant, a grunt, and a gopher (you know, go for this and go for that). Cheapskates!

### Reject Cheapskate Companies

Then, I rejected another company that offered me a no-cap bonus program (sounded pretty good on the surface), but they would not put the plan down in writing. They also offered me a base salary that was nearly 30 percent less than what I was previously receiving! They gave me the excuse that it was cheaper in that part of the country than in Southern California. Yeah, right! *Life is too short to work for cheapskate companies.*

> *Life is too short to work for cheapskate companies.*

### Cheapskates Do Not Offer Fair Deals

To top it all, they offered me only $10,000 for total relocation expenses to move halfway across the country, and I had already convinced them to increase it by 100 percent from $5,000 to $10,000. A previous company had spent a total of over $60,000 on our move (all promised expenses were covered). Adding insult to injury, that move was only one-tenth the distance of the move halfway cross-country. They said they were giving me a fair deal. Yeah, right!

### If They Won't Move You, Forget About Working for Them

To add further insult to injury, they expected us to pack all of our own household goods and haul it ourselves in a U-Haul truck! Can you see me driving a U-Haul truck cross-country in snow and ice? We had never, ever done that before throughout my entire career, and we have previously moved at least eight times on long, cross-country distances. Every other company had paid for all of our relocation expenses. All this grief, and they wanted me to prepare winning proposals to increase their total revenue by 500 percent in five years. Speaking of cheapskates, this one really took the cake!

## Number of Negotiating Results

Remember, you will receive about 50 percent or less of the negotiating results of which you counter. So, if you counter with two negotiating results, count on receiving one or even less. I usually counter with about six or seven negotiating results. Hence, I usually achieve agreement on about three of my six negotiating results in their counter-counteroffer.

### Better to Get Something Rather Than Nothing

Of the number of negotiating results you ask the hiring company to consider, include about 50 percent significant negotiating results and 50 percent less significant negotiating results. If the company cannot give you any of the significant negotiating results, almost always, they will feel obligated to capitulate on the less significant negotiating results. The message here is that *it is better to get something rather than nothing at all.*

> *It is better to get something rather than nothing at all.*

### Examples of Negotiating Results

As an example, you could ask for some of these negotiating results (these are not in any particular order of importance):

- **Significant Negotiating Results**
  - Incentive bonus plan
  - Increase in base salary
  - Increase in relocation allowance or, nowadays, to even have a relocation package at all
  - Extended temporary housing (furnished apartment rental up to six months or a year)
  - Extended travel allowance (either mileage or a leased automobile)
  - Stock options
  - Sign-on bonus
  - Gross up on relocation taxes (they pay for your taxes)
- **Less Significant Negotiating Results**
  - Cell phone and all cost of calls
  - Payment of professional dues (up to a cap of, say, $500)
  - Provision of two computers (a desktop and laptop)
  - Salary increase review in 90 days

## Worst-Case Scenario

The worst-case scenario is if the hiring company does not counter your counteroffer. That indicates the kind of people you would be working with, i.e., a bunch of chintzy folks. Unless you are hard-up or desperate, do not go to work with such chintzy people. *You should explore all counteroffers.* An employer should never ignore a job seeker's counteroffer. A company that ignores counteroffers is a lousy company. They will totally ignore you after you get on board. Drop them fast.

> *You should explore all counteroffers.*

## Your Leveraging Position

Note that the amount of "real" leverage that you possess in any negotiations is a function of how much you have to offer and how badly the hiring company wants and needs your services. If the hiring company does not need you bad enough, they will not give you many of the requested negotiating results. If they absolutely cannot do without your services, they will bend over backwards to coax you to come to work for them.

So, *if you possess "real" leveraging power, ask for the moon.* The hiring company will throw compensation, benefits, and perks your way. On the other hand, if you are not in a strong negotiating position, ask for a reasonable number of negotiating results. You may receive some concessions. However, if you don't ask, they won't give. So, ask and you shall receive.

> *If you possess "real" leveraging power, ask for the moon.*

## Strive for Leveraged Negotiations

Leverage yourself so that you can negotiate a good salary from a position of strength. *Always negotiate your offered salary.* Do not accept the first offer made to you. If you do not have a good leveraging position, take the job but start working so that you will develop some leveraging advantages for your next job search.

> *Always negotiate your offered salary.*

## Bird in Hand or Two in the Bush?

*I just got a job offer with Bank of America (BOA) as a teller today. I also interviewed with Washington Mutual (WaMu) last Tuesday. They said to call back on Friday, so I did, and I was told that they had an interview [with someone] scheduled on Tuesday (yesterday). They said they did not call back because they were still interviewing and not to think that they didn't like me.*

*I called back this morning, and I talked to the manager who said that there were more interviews; I think they just were sent more applicants. She said to hang in there and that she would personally call me back when a job offer is ready. It sounded like I would get the offer, but now, I'm not sure. I believe WaMu pays better because I have a friend who works there and the offer from BOA is less than what they got.*

*How long should I wait to get a job offer from WaMu? I told Bank of America that I could respond by Friday or next Monday.*

Graduating Senior

### Good Negotiating Position

You are in a good negotiating position. You currently have the BOA job offer in hand, which you had received today. WaMu is presently toying with you. By continuing to interview other job applicants, all they are doing is looking for a better candidate to give an offer. You need to force their hand. Tell them that you "really" want to come to work for them; however, you have an offer in-hand from BOA and that you need to give them their decision by Monday. This may shake loose an offer from WaMu.

### Negotiating is a Game of Perception

By the way, did you tell BOA that you had a pending offer from WaMu? If you did not, you should. That gets them quite nervous. They may even increase their offer to you when they realize that they may lose you. By leveraging one against the other, that is how your personal stock increases in value in the minds of both hiring managers. *Negotiating the best offer is all a game of perception.* If they perceive you as a higher-value candidate, they would offer you a sweeter deal.

> *Negotiating the best offer is all a game of perception.*

### Don't Burn Your Bridges

When Monday arrives and if you have not received an offer from WaMu, accept the BOA offer. Then, if WaMu comes through with their offer, say for example, next Wednesday, negotiate and accept that offer. Then, go back to BOA and sadly tell them that the WaMu offer had come through and that you had accepted their offer, so you now need to withdraw your acceptance of the BOA offer. Be nice about it. In other words, *do not "burn your bridges" behind you.*

You could also make an acceptance after you start working for a couple of weeks with BOA. I have seen that happen before when I had worked at HR Textron, Inc. A new employee there quit after a couple of weeks on the job to accept a better deal. He left on good terms.

> *Do not "burn your bridges" behind you.*

### Thank You Card, Note, or Email

Because I have had bad experiences with BOA in the past, I am not very high on BOA. On the other hand, since my daughter, Heather, was treated very well by WaMu and went to work for them, naturally, I am partial to WaMu and feel it is a better bank. *Perception is everything.* Hence, if you feel the same way about WaMu, then you need to try to "pull" an offer from the WaMu hiring manager. I hope you had sent the WaMu hiring manager a thank you card, note, or email. If you did, great! If you didn't, shame on you. Do it immediately if not sooner!

> *Perception is everything.*

### Go Forward!

*Bank of America (BOA) was on campus today and I spoke to the recruiter. I told him that I was recently offered a position as a teller but I had to decline it due to another offer from Washington Mutual (WaMu). He asked how much they offered me, but I did not want to disclose that amount. Is he allowed to ask me that? I told him how much more they offered which, basically, tells them what my offer was.*

*He then asked me which recruiters I spoke with, and I told him who they were. He knew both of them. He asked what part of town I live in, and then he mentioned that there was an opening nearby. I told him where my position would be, and then he immediately knew who the manager was. He asked for my contact information, and he said that he will talk to the recruiter and the district manager to see what they can do.*

*I am interested in BOA, but not as much anymore since I got the job from WaMu. If I get a better offer, should I take it? I start this Thursday at WaMu. A friend referred me to WaMu, so I don't want to back out at the last minute. Recently, I have debated if I should have taken the BOA offer since they have tuition reimbursement, and they will pay for licenses for series 6, 7, and so on. He said that they will contact me, or he will call me personally to see what they can do. I asked for his business card, and I thanked him for his time.*

Graduating Senior

## Keep Them Guessing

On your first question, "Is he allowed to ask me that?," the answer is "yes." He can ask you anything he desires. This is a free country, so he can ask you anything. However, that does not mean that you need to answer the question or give him the amount WaMu offered you. Be nice but respectfully decline to reveal any such information.

> ***Do not ever give them the amount you were offered.***

What he wanted was the amount you will make so that he can come back with a counteroffer at a slightly higher amount that you will be receiving from WaMu. What you should have said is this: "I am not disclosing what WaMu had offered me, but it was more than what BOA had offered me." Keep him guessing. *Do not ever give them the amount you were offered.*

## Do Not Prostitute Yourself

On your second question, "If I get a better offer, should I take it?," your question indicates that you are willing to prostitute yourself. You have already proven that, and now it all depends on the dollars they are willing to pay you. I am certain you have a price that would coax you away from the WaMu offer.

Accepting a counteroffer is generally frowned upon in recruiting circles. Search executives warn that executives who accept counteroffers usually lose their companies' trust and end up leaving within a year. "Nine out of 10 times, counteroffers end up being the departure platform," says Mark Lonergan, managing partner of Lonergan Richards, a Redwood City, Calif., search firm. "The people who accept find they lost points around trust, and it's more difficult to get their jobs done because they're no longer considered part of the team."[2] The lack of trust factor does not go away just because we are dealing with a recent college graduate here.

---

2   Perri Capell, "When Taking a Counteroffer Can Beat Going Elsewhere," taken from CareerJournal.com, The Wall Street Journal Executive Career Site, at http://www.careerjournal.com/salaryhiring/negotiate/20050329-capell.html on 1/1/2006.

## Much of Leveraging is Perception

Here is the problem you will get yourself into should you prostitute yourself. Because you had turned down BOA for WaMu, they feel rejected and unhappy that you did not go with them. Now, when they wave a few more dollars in front of your eyes and you take it, they know you are a prostitute and, therefore, they will dislike you even more.

However, when you go to work for them, you will have lost your leveraging capability and will now be under their control. *Remember, much of leveraging is perception.* Because you have proven yourself as a prostitute to them, they will not treat you as well as they would had you accepted their first offer over WaMu. Do you see the dynamics here?

> *Remember, much of leveraging is perception.*

## Know the Dynamics Involved with Negotiations

When you withdraw your acceptance of the WaMu offer, you will make them unhappy by appearing to prostitute yourself. Should they increase their offer to beat the new BOA offer and you decide to stay with them, they will then have you under their control. However, they will feel differently about you because you showed yourself as a figurative prostitute. Do you see the dynamics involved here?

## Negotiate Aggressively on the First Go-around

So, how do you avoid appearing as a prostitute by both BOA and WaMu, yet negotiate successfully? You do this by applying your leveraging and negotiating strategies to the hilt on the first go-around. If you recall, you did not negotiate to the hilt on the first go-around. Instead, once BOA said they would not increase their offer, you then accepted the WaMu offer. You could have aggressively negotiated with WaMu to get them to increase their offer or even negotiated other benefits such as getting them to pay tuition assistance for your master's program. As I recall, however, you did not do that. Hence, you missed an opportunity to sweeten the WaMu deal.

## Re-negotiating Your Salary Puts You in a Very Precarious Position

By attempting to re-negotiate now after the company deals are closed, you put yourself in a very precarious position, i.e., appearing as a figurative prostitute. No matter what company you go with now, by attempting to reopen negotiations, you end up looking bad in both companies' eyes. Do you understand the situation in which you find yourself?

### Avoid "Buyer's Remorse" and Appearing Wishy-washy

Whenever you make a decision, you should take it and not look backwards. Do not entertain "buyer's remorse." Take the first decision you make and move forward. By being indecisive at this point, you just appear wishy-washy. Both BOA and WaMu will see that flaw in your character. Instead, go forward.

> ### *Do not entertain "buyer's remorse."*

Move onward and upward. *Do not entertain "buyer's remorse."* If you now "change horses in the middle of the stream" and appear wishy-washy, you will repeat that shortcoming throughout your life. Instead, go forward!

### *Receiving and Negotiating a Good Offer*

The moral of the story is this:

- Never give your desired salary number until the hiring company is ready to make you an offer.
- Never accept the first offer.
- Everything is negotiable. Ask and you shall receive.
- You are worth exactly what you accept.

Therefore, negotiate with confidence! The following chapters will "peel back the onion" and show you exactly what you need to do to receive the salary and other benefits you so rightly deserve.

*Chapter 2*

# Negotiating Job Offers

---

*Request a face-to-face meeting to review the details of the job. In person, you'll have the opportunity to read the decision maker's reactions and adjust your strategy accordingly. Focus on your worth, rather than your needs. Emphasize your value to the company and your desire to be compensated competitively. Use data to back up your request.[3]*

Abridged: Coloradan Online

## The Last 100-yard Dash

*The interview went extremely well. He told me I did a great job. When I asked if he saw a fit, he answered, "yes"! However, he did tell me that he has another candidate who is equally qualified, and he will need to make a decision from his "gut," as he is under pressure to make a decision quickly.*

*I am planning on mailing a thank-you note today. Would it be appropriate to go beyond the thank you as far as advocating for this position or stating that I feel I am qualified? I know he will be making a decision soon.*

CSUSM 2005 Graduate

### Analysis of the Situation

Congratulations on your interview going well! Yes, it is appropriate to go beyond the thank you note in advocating for this position. However, be aware of these things:

---

[3] No Author Indicated, "Salary Negotiating Tip," abridged from the *Coloradan Online*, quoted from *The Career News*, Vol. 5, Issue 27, July 11, 2005.

- He is already sold on your capabilities, qualifications, talents, achievements, and motivation for the job. He said you did a great job in the interview, and you were a good FIT.
- You are equally qualified with your only other competitor.
- The choice will be made soon between you two.
- His choice will be made on "gut" feel.
- So, his choice will be made on who he feels will work better with him.
- Stating that you feel you are qualified for the job will do nothing to enhance your position. He already knows and believes that you are well qualified for the job.
- What you need to do is to *appeal to his male ego.*
- Do not talk about yourself. That will focus your appeal inward. Do not give any indications of self-centeredness or selfishness.

> *Appeal to his male ego.*

- Instead, *focus your appeal outward. Talk about him and the company.* Talk about how anxious you are to start working for him and that you look forward with great anticipation to support his vision for the company. Talk about how you have always wanted to work for a boss like him. Talk about the plans you have in assisting him to grow the business. Be ready with some points of those plans should he call you by phone and ask you to delineate your plans for helping the business grow.

> *Focus your appeal outward. Talk about him and the company.*

### Focus On the Hiring Manager

Do you see what I am driving at here? Keep the writing or conversation away from yourself. Do not say anything more about your capabilities, talents, qualifications, or desire for the job. He is already sold on that.

### Gut Feel, Vibrations, Chemistry, and Synch

What he is not totally sold on yet is the gut feel, the vibrations, the chemistry, being in-synch, and the "yes, you are the one I want to hire" feeling. If that were so, he would have said that he wanted you instead of saying there is an "equally qualified candidate."

## Appeal to the Ego

This is not to imply that you have lost the job. I believe he truly is in a tough-decision mode (quandary, if you may). So, the one of you final two candidates who can successfully stroke his male ego (without making it obvious, of course) better than the other is the one he will select to make an offer.

## She Who Wants It Most, Wins

Whichever of you who wants this job the most will come out ahead on this final competitive effort. Of course, if you make the effort and she does not because she does not have a job coach, then you win and she loses. That makes sense; does it not?

What you do in the next 24 hours is crucial to capturing this job. Good luck!

## *Declining and Accepting Offers*

*How does one courteously decline a position offered at an interview? I have been offered two positions (Yeah!), but I have to make a decision and refuse one of the two offers. Your feedback is appreciated!*

CSUSM Alumnus

## Always Get Offers In Writing

I assume the offer at the interview was made verbally to you. Your first reaction after showing surprise and delight should be, "Would you please put that offer in writing?" Leave it at that. However, if the hiring manager presses you to accept the offer verbally at that moment, say, "After I receive your written offer, I will compare it against my other alternatives, make a decision, and let you know my decision. But your offer sounds really good!"

## Never Rush to Any Acceptance Decision

*Do not rush into making any decision.* Unless you are wondering where your next meal is coming from, never make a decision on the spot to accept an initial offer. Always give it and you some time to cool off so that you will have the necessary amount of time to think about it in the right frame of mind.

> *Do not rush into making any decision.*

## Don't Make This Mistake

A friend of mine had received a good job offer over the phone from the hiring manager. He made the mistake of telling the hiring manager that he would let him know of his decision in a couple of days. He should have said that he would need a week to 10 days to make his decision after he did some research, weighed it against his other alternatives, and talked with his wife about it.

## Hiring Company Wants Quick Decision

The hiring company usually wants to accelerate your decision making process for fear of losing you to one of their competing companies. Hence, they will tell you that they need you ASAP. It is your responsibility to extend the negotiations process as long as possible without turning off the hiring manager. You never know when an even better opportunity will present itself from another company.

## Always Decline Offers in Writing

*Always courteously decline an offer in writing, never verbally over the phone.* By putting it in writing, you will be able to review and polish the letter of rejection so that it sounds really good while delineating all of your reasons as to why you accepted the other offer.

When you reject an offer verbally, what comes out of your mouth is what it is you said no matter how bad it may sound. That approach is too risky. Additionally, a letter can be read and re-read by the hiring company and its upper management. Others can read it and may urge their management to come back with an even better counteroffer.

> *Always courteously decline offers in writing, never verbally over the phone.*

## Never Reject an Offer

In your letter of rejection, note that I said you should delineate the reasons why you had accepted the other offer. Never write in your letter of rejection as to why you are rejecting their offer. Your explanation will only come across negatively to them, and any idea of a counteroffer would probably be negated.

## Always Say You Accepted Another Offer

When you delineate the reasons why you had accepted the other offer, it provides them with a baseline to work from should they decide to prepare a counteroffer to you. They would know the reasons why you had accepted the other offer. All they need to do is to give you more than the reasons you had stated in your letter to sweeten the counteroffer.

### Always Get Counteroffers in Writing

If the hiring manager or human resource (HR) specialist calls you over the phone to give you a counteroffer, ask them to please put it in writing. After you receive the letter, you will study it, compare it against your other alternatives, talk it over with your spouse or significant other, and then get back with them.

## *Always Accept Offers in Writing*

Now, when accepting the other offer, again, do not do so verbally over the phone. *Always accept an offer in writing*. However, before you accept the offer, always write a letter of negotiations to the hiring company to encourage them to sweeten the offer.

> *Always accept an offer in writing.*

### When You Have Leverage, Do Negotiate!

If you have an excellent work history, you have leverage. For example, if you have had some solid jobs managing hundreds of apartment complexes, you have leverage. That is a far cry from working in fast-food restaurants and other similar low-leverage jobs. You can ask for and receive more than what you were initially offered. However, if you do not ask for more, you will not receive more. So, ask!

### Example of a Negotiating Letter

Here is an example of a letter written by a friend of mine:

> *It was great speaking with you on Tuesday. I am very excited to come to work for the XYZ Corporation. Before I do that, however, I was hoping that you would consider increasing my annual salary by $5,000 to compensate for the significant cost burden that I must bear for medical and dental coverage at XYZ.*
>
> *The cost for medical and dental coverage at XYZ is about double what I currently pay at ABC, Inc. Hence, I would be receiving less net income at XYZ than I am currently receiving from ABC. I was hoping to earn about the same or even a little more by my transition from ABC to XYZ. Please feel free to contact me at your convenience to discuss this matter.*

## Always Negotiate Cordially

Remember, the company that you may first want to reject may be the one that will come back with much more pay and several more benefits than the one that you originally wanted to accept. However, you will never know that until you negotiate both offers instead of just rejecting one and accepting the other. Just as in purchasing real estate, unless you have fallen in love with the house, *do not make your decision without the necessary and sufficient negotiations.*

> *Do not make your decision without the necessary and sufficient negotiations.*

## Negotiating a Vacation during the Hiring Process

*Is it unprofessional to negotiate a vacation in the hiring process? My question regards those of us who would like to travel a bit before diving right into the business world. I will be graduating in December and then traveling for two months to Australia and Southeast Asia.*

*What is the proper etiquette in relaying this intention to potential employers without giving them the wrong idea about me (I am not a slacker)? Thank you very much for any ideas you could give me.*

A College Student

No, it is not unprofessional and it is okay to negotiate a vacation during the hiring process. However, you should have a compelling reason to negotiate such a vacation during the hiring process. The hiring manager must want very much for you to come to work for them. In this situation, you possess what is called *leverage. Leverage is defined as the increased means of accomplishing some purpose* (in this case, getting to take the vacation). However, if the hiring manager has other equally qualified, potential candidates ready to assume the job you are seeking, then you do not possess enough leverage to attempt to negotiate successfully a vacation during the hiring process.

> *Leverage is defined as the increased means of accomplishing some purpose.*

## Inform the Employer During the Offer-Negotiation Process

The best time to inform the employer about your intended two-month vacation prior to starting work is during the offer-negotiation process. If most companies were anything like Enterprise Rent-A-Car, they would be amenable to your taking the two months off before starting to work. They would just move your start date to some time in March. Hey, why don't you go to work for Enterprise Rent-A-Car!

### Critical Jobs Would Present a Problem

Usually, the only time you would have a problem is if you were filling a critical position that requires you to be there, say, yesterday. Then, the company may be a little reluctant to allow you to take the time off before starting the new job.

However, as a newly minted BSBA degree holder, the hiring company probably will not offer you a critical job with the need for an immediate start date. Therefore, have fun in Australia (down under) and Southeast Asia!

## How Would I Know That an Out-of-State Job is a Good One?

*I may have a potential job offer as a marketing manager after graduation. It would be a fantastic opportunity, but it would require me to work in Arizona. If the money and experience are acceptable, I would definitely move. From everything that I have heard, it sounds like a great job. How do I go about asking what level is the salary? In the meantime, should I also continue to look into internships and other job opportunities? What if, during the time before graduation, I find another opportunity? How would I tell the current potential job offeror that I have decided to work for another company and still be able to encourage them to keep me in mind in the future?*

Graduating Senior

### Salary Discussion

If you are that far along on landing this job, I'm surprised that the salary subject hasn't yet been broached by the hiring company. By now, they should have asked you for your desired salary range and your salary history. If they make you an offer, then you can point-blank ask them what salary comes with the job.

### Moving to Arizona

If they hire you for this marketing manager position, take it and move to Arizona. Arizona is not that bad of a place to live. Granted, not many places can beat San Diego County. However, the Phoenix area is growing by leaps-and-bounds. Apparently, many people have uprooted their families and moved to Arizona, which indicates that it is a desirable place to live and work. You are young and do not have too many responsibilities to keep you tied to San Diego. If you find that the job is not that great, you can always move back to Southern California in a year or so.

## Keep Your Job Searching Effort Going

In the meantime, you should continue your job searching effort. Never stop your effort until you have a written offer-in-hand, and you have accepted the offer. Even then, sometimes, hiring companies retract offers before you start working for them. Hence, it is a good idea to keep your job searching effort going until you actually start working for that company. Then, you can quit searching.

## Keep Your Options Open

If you accept an offer and then, later, you receive an even better offer, take the better offer, run, and never look back. Just write the first company a nice letter and tell them that you had another offer that you just could not refuse. However, forget about ever going back to that company to work for them in the future. There are enough companies out there that you don't need to be focused on only one company. So, don't worry about it. Move forward, onward, and upward.

### *Accepting An Offer From a Company With "Trashy" and "Risqué" Products*

*I recently had an interview with a footwear company for a position as a sales manager. A relative of mine helped me obtain the interview. The position has great benefits with an adequate salary. This footwear company offered me the position, and I would begin this summer. The offices are located in a city quite a distance from where I currently live, so I would have to move.*

*I really liked everyone I met in the company, but I did run into one problem. The actual line of shoes appears to be very "trashy." They cater to dancers and are a little risqué. Should I accept a position if I do not necessarily believe in the product?*

*The position is in the right industry that I am looking for, but I am afraid the reputation of the footwear line can affect my future prospects in the industry. Does the position and the duties written on a resume make more of an impact than the company?*

Job Seeker

### Combinations of Position and Company

There are four combinations of position and company:

- Lackluster company and a lackluster position
- Top-notch company but a lackluster position
- Lackluster company but a top-notch position
- Top-notch company and a top-notch position

To help build a solid resume, you should seek companies and positions that fit bullet number four.

### Bullets That Sell

Though you may write a sentence under each position that describes the duties of that position, you should keep the job description, duties, and responsibilities to a minimum. Instead, under that position, you should include one to five bullets that show your superior performance, outstanding results, significant achievements, and noteworthy accomplishments. These bullets are what will sell you to the reader. These bullets must "grab" the reader's attention, "hook" the reader's interest, and "pack a punch." If you do that, you will have many calls for interviews.

### Bottom Line: Listen to Your Gut

If you do not believe in the product or products you will be selling, you should give serious thought as to whether you should accept the position. You will not sell at your peak if you do not believe in the product. The bottom line is that you should *listen to your "gut."* You will seldom if ever go wrong by listening to your gut.

> *Listen to your "gut."*

Ultimately, candidates should accept jobs they feel will be satisfying and challenging, and not necessarily because they pay the most. This means taking "the stomach test" when a final offer is on the table, says Mr. Mark Edwards, chairman of Compensia, an executive-compensation consulting firm based in San Jose, California. "You have to ask what your gut feels like," he says. "Do you like the company, its prospects, the offer, the people there and its vision for the future, and are you ready to ride the bucking bronco?"[4]

---

4   Ms. Perri Capell, "How Does Your Current Pay Stack Up Against a New Offer?," *CareerJournal.com*, The Wall Street Journal Executive Career Site, http://www.careerjournal.com/salaryhiring/negotiate/20040825-capell.html, extracted on 1/1/2006. Ms. Capell is a senior correspondent for *CareerJournal.com*. She can be reached at frances.capell@dowjones.com.

## Informal Job Offer by Former Boss

*A former boss has informally offered me a job after I graduate. I work well with him and would like to discuss opportunities. When is a good time to contact him and seriously discuss any possibilities?*

Graduating Senior

### Do Not Procrastinate

Do not let too much time go by because he may either:

(1)  Forget that he made you that informal offer

(2)  Start thinking that you are not very interested in his offer to you

You also need to decide whether this job and company comprise the best avenue for your career. Is this his own small business or is he a boss in a large company?

### Get Things Going Early

If you will graduate in May, it is not too early to get the ball rolling. If this is what you really want to do, I suggest you set up a meeting with him and discuss the job in detail.

### Most Important Criterion

Throughout the years, I have found that *the most important criterion as to how well you do in a job depends on for whom you work*. It is good for your career to work for someone who has full faith and confidence in your job performance.

> **The most important criterion as to how well you do in a job depends on for whom you work.**

## 11 Commandments for Smart Negotiating

Mr. Lee E. Miller is the author of *Get More Money On Your Next Job: 25 Proven Strategies for Getting More Money, Better Benefits, and Greater Job Security,* (McGraw-Hill, 1998). He said, "There are 11 basic commandments to help you negotiate the best possible deal in any economic climate when changing jobs, whether internally or with a new company. They are:

1. Be prepared.
2. Recognize that employment negotiations are different.
3. Understand your needs and those of the employer.
4. Understand the dynamics of the particular negotiations.
5. Never lie, but use the truth to your advantage.
6. Understand the role fairness plays in the process.
7. Use uncertainty to your advantage.
8. Be creative.
9. Focus on your goals, not on winning.
10. Know when to quit bargaining.
11. Never forget that employment is an ongoing relationship.

Understanding these principles will allow you to effectively negotiate the terms of your new job in good times and in bad. Once you are hired, do your job well and continually seek out new challenges. As you take on added responsibilities and learn new skills, there will be opportunities to negotiate further improvements."[5] These are excellent commandments to abide by when you negotiate your salary with a hiring company.

## Do Not Slow Down

### Not a Time to Relax

Even if you are awaiting an offer from a company, do not sit back and relax. Continue your job search with a vengeance…like it was the first day of your job searching activities. Keep active in all areas:

- Networking
- Searching websites on the Internet
- Polishing your resume and cover letter
- Looking for newspaper ads
- Reading job searching articles

---

5  Lee E. Miller, "Eleven Commandments for Smart Negotiating," Taken from the *CareerJournal.com*, The Wall Street Journal Executive Career Site, http://www.careerjournal.com/salaryhiring/negotiate/20030624-miller.html on 1/1/2006.

- Taking seminars at the Career Center
- Sending out tailored, customized resumes/cover letters
- Honing your computer skills
- Many, many other job-searching-related activities

### The Ideal Situation

The ideal situation is to receive several job offers within a short time interval of each other. This way, you will be able to leverage one against the other during negotiations so that you can maximize your offers. So, keep churning the pot.

# *Chapter 3*
# Determining Prevailing Salaries

*You're about to negotiate a salary with a prospective employer, but you have no idea what the going rate is. What do you do? One strategy is to check pay-comparison Internet sites such as salary.com and salaryexpert.com. The Web sites show salary ranges for hundreds of job titles. For instance, one says pharmaceutical-sales reps make an average $49,000 a year. The sites say they gather the information from surveys of corporate human-resources departments. In some cases, it's the same data employers use to set pay scales.*[6]

Karen Frangos

## Effective Salary Negotiations

*When is the proper time to negotiate what you believe to be a fair salary and what are good ways of going about this without sounding money hungry? Upon going into the interview, if you are unsure about what the salary is going to be, how do you go about finding this out?*

### Two Appropriate Times to Negotiate Your Salary

There are two appropriate times to negotiate your salary. The *first time* is when and if the hiring manager brings up salary during your interviews. *Do not ever bring up salary before your interviewer brings it up.* When the interviewer broaches the subject, ask him/her if he/she is making you an offer. If he/she is, then you can talk/negotiate your salary. If he/she says, "no," he/she is

> *Do not ever bring up salary before your interviewer brings it up.*

---

6    Karen Frangos, "Know the Going Rate Before Talking Salary," From *The Wall Street Journal Online*, CareerJournal.com, extracted on 1/1/2006.

not making you an offer, then, say you will be happy to discuss salary when he/she is prepared to make you an offer. The **second time** that would be appropriate to negotiate salary is when you receive an offer letter. Then, negotiate to the hilt but in a nice manner, of course.

## Do Your Homework

If you are unsure about what your salary should be, you can get a better handle of it by doing the following:

- *Research.* Perform salary research on the Internet. You can find many salary websites by going to "Ask Jeeves at http://www.ask.com." Find out what salaries newly minted college graduates in similar career fields receive.

- *Analyze.* Determine what bare minimum salary you will accept and what you really want for a salary. These two extremes comprise the range of your salary requirements. However, what you are really worth is what you accept, and that would be your lowest threshold figure.

- *Negotiate.* When the hiring company initiates salary discussions, they will ask you for your salary history and your desired salary range. When they ask you for these, ask them what salary range they have for this job. You need to get an idea of their salary range that they are willing to offer you. The mid-point of that range is usually where they want to end up.

## Know Exactly What You are Going to Do

If you have done sufficient homework and are well prepared, you can conduct effective salary negotiations. Never go into salary negotiations not knowing exactly:

- What salary they will offer you
- What salary range they are willing to give you
- What salary others of similar background, experience, and education are receiving
- What salary you want
- What salary you will accept and receive
- What salary you are worth, which is exactly what you will accept

If you know all of these things, you will not risk leaving any money on the negotiating table.

## Dealing with Salary History

*Upon sending in my resume to a company and being called in for an interview, how do I omit including past earnings in the job application? Is it acceptable to write on the application "Will be discussed during the interview"?*

Student

### Do Not Give Your Salary History Before the Interview

You do not want to give your salary history before you receive an interview. This is because companies use salary histories to weed out highly-paid candidates. Some companies also use this information to determine the salary ranges of all people in your area doing similar work. This knowledge helps them maintain the "upper hand" in salary negotiations with you.

### Get Them to Pay You What You are Worth

Once you go in for an interview, then it is okay to reveal your salary history only when they are ready to make you an offer. When you interview, you have an opportunity to prove to the interviewers that you are worth the high salary you command. Once the hiring manager is impressed with you, a high salary is not as much of a problem. If you are in great demand, the hiring company will pay you whatever you are worth. *Remember, whatever you are worth is what you will accept.*

> *Whatever you are worth is what you will accept.*

### Filling Out the Application Forms

When I know a company wants me badly enough, I do not fill out the application before I go in for the interview. When they ask for it in the interview, I tell them that I will type it out ASAP and get it to them post haste. They are usually receptive to this approach. Of course, if they were not hotly pursuing me, they would use my not completing and submitting the application as their reason for discontinuing any more discussions. Oh, well!

## How to Find Out About Prevailing Salaries

*What is the best way to find out what your peers are being paid and/or what a competitive wage/salary is for your industry?*

Employee

### Go to Ask Jeeves and Do Some Research

Go to Ask Jeeves at http://www.ask.com and do some research on entry-level salaries for the job you seek. Find out what the going rate is in the location that you desire to work. Through your research, you should be able to determine the range of salaries for entry-level jobs in the discipline you are in and for the location in which you will be working.

### Establish Your Desired Personal Salary Range

Then, determine exactly what you desire for a salary and what the lowest salary amount below which you absolutely cannot and will not go. These two figures give you your personal salary range that you desire.

### Compare Your Desires to Prevailing Industry Ranges

Now, compare the prevailing industry salary range against your personal salary range. If they coincide or have an area of overlap, you are in good shape. If your personal range is below the industry range with no overlap whatsoever, you need to have an attitude adjustment. Chances are you have a very low self-image and self-esteem.

### Adjust Your Desires to the Prevailing Industry Range

On the other hand, if your personal range is above the industry range with no overlap at all, that indicates that either you have no concept of reality or you have an over-inflated ego and think you are worth much more than you are actually worth. Again, you need an attitude adjustment. Lower your personal range to have some overlap with the industry range.

### Terri Levine Writes

Terri Levine, president of Comprehensive Coaching U, in an article in *The Wall Street Journal* titled "The Top 7 Signs of Self-Sabotaging Behaviors," lists seven signs of self-sabotaging behaviors as follows:

1   Focusing on what is not working or not right
2.   Being stuck in fear
3.   Feeling you have no value
4.   Comparison of self to others
5.   Meeting goals and then losing them

6.  You chase away relationships

7.  Having no purpose[7]

So, we should avoid getting trapped in these self-sabotaging behaviors and adjust our desires to have some overlap with the prevailing industry ranges.

### Develop a Personal Mission in Life and Pursue Your Passions

You must not wallow in these counterproductive behaviors. Instead, focus on what is working and right. Work on your self-confidence. Learn to like yourself and feel that you are worth a lot. Refrain from comparing yourself to those who are way above-and-beyond you. As you accomplish goals (no matter how small they are), relish in those little victories. Work on your network and cultivate good, meaningful relationships. Above all, develop goals and a plan to accomplish them. *Develop a personal mission in life and pursue your passions.*

> *Develop a personal mission in life and pursue your passions.*

### You are Worth Exactly What You Accept

Now, all of this discussion is fine and dandy. That's ivory tower talk. However, *what you are really worth is what you accept, or you are worth exactly what you accept, or you are only worth what you accept.* That's getting down to reality. If you accept anything below the industry range, that's what you are worth. Worse yet, if you actually accept a salary below what you had set as your lowest limit in your personal salary range, that's all you are worth, which is worse than worst! You probably will be living in poverty.

### Don't Accept a Salary Below the Poverty Level

Don't live in poverty. *The average poverty figure in the United States is $30,000 or below per year of gross income.* Do not accept anything below the poverty level. Why do you go to college and graduate if you will accept a poverty salary level? Trade workers will be making more than you would be making. College graduates should make more money than do

> *The average poverty figure in the United States is $30,000 or below per year of gross income.*

---

7  Terri Levine, President, Comprehensive Coaching U—as seen in *The Wall Street Journal* is the author of bestseller, *Work Yourself Happy & Coaching for an Extraordinary Life.* www.coachinginstruction.com.

blue-collar workers. Don't insult yourself, your college, and all college graduates by accepting a poverty level salary. Expect the best and get it!

## Seek to Receive the Industry Average or Better

Average starting salary offers are on the rise for new college graduates with bachelor's degrees according to a survey by the National Association of Colleges and Employers (NACE). The NACE prepared the data in the following table, which indicates what a degree is worth and what are starting salaries for the class of 2005. If you are negotiating a job offer, get to know and understand these average salary survey data from the NACE. These figures will help you negotiate a better deal.

### WHAT'S A DEGREE WORTH?
**Here are some average starting salaries for the class of 2005:**

| MAJOR | STARTING | VS. 2004 |
|---|---|---|
| Chemical engineering | $54,256 | +4.3% |
| Electrical engineering | $52,009 | +2.5% |
| Computer engineering | $51,496 | -2.0% |
| Computer science | $51,292 | +2.6% |
| Mechanical engineering | $51,046 | +4.1% |
| Aerospace engineering* | $50,701 | +9.0% |
| Industrial Engineering | $49,541 | +1.8% |
| Accounting | $43,809 | +3.9% |
| Information sciences | $43,732 | -0.8% |
| Civil engineering | $43,462 | +4.0% |
| Economics/finance | $42,802 | +5.1% |
| Business administration | $39,448 | +3.2% |
| Marketing | $37,832 | +6.0% |
| Liberal arts | $30,337 | +4.2% |

Source:
National Association of Colleges and Employers
*Also aeronautical and astronautical engineering degrees

## Do Not Go Below the Poverty Level!

All business graduates should be able to earn an annual starting salary between $30,000 to $44,000. The average student should easily be able to receive $36,000 per annum. If you accept less, that's what you're really worth, no more. Remember, *if you accept below $30,000 per annum, you will be receiving a poverty-level salary, so do not go below $30,000 per annum!*

## Strive to Be a Person Who "Walks on Water"

> ***If you accept below $30,000 per annum, you will be receiving a poverty-level salary, so do not go below $30,000 per annum!***

If you are an average student, you should be able to obtain $36,000–$40,000 per annum. The average BSBA graduate should be able to obtain $39,500 per annum. If you are a super student, you should be able to receive between $40,000–$44,000 per annum. If you walk on water, you should be able to get over $44,000 per annum.

## Maximize Your Starting Salary!

As usual, engineering and computer science graduates will receive the most money ($49,000–$55,000 per annum!), which can be over $10,000 per year more than highest-paid business and finance graduates. Hence, it pays to work hard to pass all of those math, physics, chemistry, engineering, and computer science courses. Now, go out there and maximize your starting salary by proving your worth and negotiating to the hilt!

## Another Cut of the Survey

"Employers tell us that the economy is improving, and likewise, more positions are open for new college graduates," explains Andrea J. Koncz, NACE's Employment Information Manager. Majors topping the list also boast significant annual earnings boosts—accounting ($44,564), management trainee ($35,811), software design and development ($53,729), and design/construction engineering ($47,048).[8]

These average salary levels (shown in the following table) provide tremendous opportunities for college graduates this year. Go out there and get what you so rightly deserve. If you don't seek it, you won't get it. So, seek it and get it. Remember, do not accept an annual salary below $30,000.

---

8    AOL Research & Learn: Online Campus—"Need a Job? Good News—Prospects and Paychecks Increase," article by Gina LaGuardia, 2005-04-21 12:11:02.

## Top 10 Jobs for 2004–05 Graduates

| Job Function | Average Salary Offer |
|---|---|
| Software Design & Development | $53,729 |
| Consulting | $49,781 |
| Design/Construction Engineering | $47,058 |
| Financial/Treasury Analysis | $45,596 |
| Accounting (Private) | $44,564 |
| Accounting (Public) | $41,039 |
| Sales | $37,130 |
| Management Trainee (Entry-Level Mgmt.) | $35,811 |
| Teaching | $29,733 |

**Source:** Spring 2005 Salary Survey, National Association of Colleges & Employers (NACE). All data is for bachelor's degree candidates. Rankings are based on number of offers reported.

# Chapter 4

# Negotiating a Salary—Part 1

*I just wanted to say thank you for all of your advice regarding my situation with my upcoming job in my father's company. I used many of the tools you prescribed in negotiating my salary. I shared with my father a couple of your emails containing topics that needed to be addressed with my position.*

*We had a very good discussion and developed a salary package that I am very excited about. My father and I opened up a line of communication that has no boundaries. We can and will discuss any topic, thought, and emotion. The only problem is that I cannot wait to finish school in May and start working.*

*My start date is June 1st, and I am ready to begin the learning process. This time it is not school (yeah!). I think you are a good teacher and thank you for being part of my educational experience at CSUSM.*

BSBA Alumnus
CSUSM

## Salary History, Salary Ranges, and Salary Requirement

### Do Not Give Companies Your Salary History

First, do not ever give any company your salary history until after they will make you an offer. Giving salary history on your resume is a no-no, even if they ask for it in the ad. Even if they say in the ad that you will not be considered if you do not include your salary history in your resume, do not include it.

### Why Companies Want Your Salary History

If you have a great resume and track record, they would be interested in you no matter what…unless they have published a phony ad, of course. Companies ask you for your salary history to generate statistics to determine what the industry averages are and what the salary increase rate is per year. Some companies will publish phony ads and ask you to give them your salary history just for developing such statistics.

### Available Salary Range, Your Desired Salary Range, and Salary Requirement

If, at the end of your interview, the interviewer asks you for your desired salary range, ask the interviewer if he/she is making you an offer. If the interview says "no," then tell him/her that you will reveal your desired salary requirement only when they are ready to make you an offer.

An alternative approach would be to immediately throw the question back at the interviewer by asking, "What range of salary do you have available to offer for this job?" Tell the interviewer that if he/she gives you the available salary range, then you will give him/her your desired salary requirement.

### Salary Negotiations

If the interviewer asks you what salary range would be acceptable to you, do not ever give him/her an acceptable salary range. If you do, he/she will make you an offer at the bottom of your acceptable range. After all, you are indicating that you would accept anything between x and y. So, they feel perfectly justified in offering you x instead of y.

> *Do not ever give your bottom salary number.*

Instead, what you should do is to give them the top annual salary number of your acceptable range and immediately tell the interviewer that you are "very flexible." Another approach is to give the interviewer the mid-range salary number and say that is what you absolutely need. *Do not ever give your bottom salary number*. You absolutely cannot and will not go below this annual salary.

### Your Worth: You are Worth Only What You Accept

Remember this maxim: *You are worth exactly what you accept.* If you accept $35K per year, then you are worth only $35K per year. You may be the same person but five minutes later accept a $43K per year salary, then you are worth $43K per year, not $35K per year, and that's only five minutes later!

*You are worth only what you accept.* So, if you lack confidence in yourself and accept the first offer made to you, that is all you are worth…not a penny more. *Only if you are hard up, starving,*

> *Only if you are hard up, starving, and do not know where your next meal is coming from should you ever accept the first offer.*

*and do not know where your next meal is coming from should you ever accept the first offer.*

Hence, if you have a lot to offer, if they want you badly, if you have money in the bank, and if you possess a good track record and a leveraged position, you should never accept the first offer. Tell them that you will need a week or two to evaluate it against the other offers you possess or will soon receive.

If you think the hiring company will laugh in your face if you asked for $43K per year, then they probably will laugh in your face. However, *if you are confident in your worth, you will look the hiring manager straight in the eyes and tell him with a poker face what you are worth.* You should show him that you are worth it. You should make him feel that he will receive his money's worth by hiring you.

> **If you are confident in your worth, you will look the hiring manager straight in the eyes and tell him with a poker face what you are worth.**

If you need to work much overtime, you will. If you need to travel often, you will. You will produce top quality products. You will make the company money and help it grow. You will help him be successful in his job.

## You Get What You Expect

*You must expect the best and get it. If you do not expect the best, you will never get the best.* If you think, believe, and act like you are worth $54,852 per year, then you are worth that much. On the other hand, if you think and believe you are worth only $35,000 per year, then that is all you are worth. *You will act out what you believe.*

> **You must expect the best and get it. If you do not expect the best, you will never get the best.**

Do you think you are only in the 25 percentile of all job seekers? Do you think you are in the 50 percentile of all job seekers? Do you think you are in the 75 percentile of all job seekers? I always believe and know that I reside in the top 95 percentile of all job seekers. You can do the same. Only you can determine what percentile in which you reside. Think about it.

## On Being a Better Negotiator

Do you want to be a better negotiator? Mariette Edwards, business and career strategist, consultant, speaker, and writer, wrote that the best negotiators…

> **You will act out what you believe.**

- Aim high. They don't settle at the outset for asking for less than what they want.

- Gather information.

- Listen.

- Know their subject matter.

- Read signals. They are adept at interpreting clues about what the other side wants and needs.

- Ask good questions.

- Express themselves well.

- Think clearly under pressure.

- Put personal integrity first.

- Prepare. Prepare. Prepare.

- Knowledge is power! Spend time getting clear on what you want before beginning any negotiation process.[9]

## More on Not Accepting the First Offer

### Drag Out the Negotiations

Please understand that when I say not to accept the first offer, I do not mean that you should make a counteroffer immediately upon receiving that offer. *Try to drag out the negotiations process as long as possible.* I let one of the companies that made me a pretty good offer sit for three weeks until they finally called me asking if I was going to accept the offer or not.

I told the HR manager who called me that I would be back with them within three days. The three-week wait gave me time to strategize and to figure out exactly what I wanted to negotiate with them. The three-week wait also put a panic into the hiring company's management because they really wanted to bring me on board.

> *Try to drag out the negotiations process as long as possible.*

---

9    Mariette Edwards, "Negotiations 101: Start With What You Want," extracted on 9/14/2005 from *net-temps.com*, Net-Temps, Inc.

## Counteroffer Letter

I documented my counteroffer in a letter and emailed it (as an attachment) to the HR manager within three days. She called me within a day after receiving my counteroffer and started throwing the following things at me including:

- An un-asked-for increase in my stock options
- Sign-on bonus
- Maximum house moving expenses paid including before and after bonuses upon selling our old home
- Full-up on the purchase of our new home (they paid all of the points and taxes)
- Six months of hotel bills paid
- Six months of a leased automobile
- All-expenses-paid cell phone
- Two computers (a laptop and a desktop)
- Payment of all professional dues

## Leveraging Power

See, the key here is that the hiring company must want you badly enough to bend over backwards to coax you to come to work for them. When they are in that situation, you have maximum leverage power over them. You can just about ask for anything, and they will give it to you.

## Don't Go Over the Line; Know When to Back Off

However, I realized I went over the line when I had asked for a one-year employment contract, i.e., if I was fired or laid off before then that they would pay for outplacement consultant costs. The HR manager said, "Are you thinking of not being with us in less than a year?" I immediately backpedaled, told her to disregard that request, and quickly moved on to the next item. See, I *know when to back off.*

> **Know when to back off.**

## Performance

That was a good job because I was able to get my department to prepare winning proposals that booked $1.3 billion of new business. However, because it is such a large amount of bookings, I cut it in half and only show $650 million of bookings for my bullet in my resume. I do possess the documentation to prove the $1.3 billion, however.

## Payoff for Hard Work

My employment at that company lasted for only three years and three months because they kept selling off divisions in which I had worked. For that three-year and three-month job, I was able to realize over $1 million for my stock options upon cashing them in. Hence, even though it was not a long-term job as I had hoped it would be, it was well worth the time that I was employed there despite having worked about 3,000 hours of free overtime for the 3.25-year period that I was there.

## Sample Negotiating Letter

### You Must Ask for Increases

Shown below is an example of a negotiating letter that someone had used successfully. The names, companies, places, and dollar amounts were changed to keep from revealing identities. Notice that, if you do not ask, you will not receive. The person who wrote this letter was provided with a $15K salary increase plus other benefits as discussed below.

### If You Have Leverage, Use It

Remember, *as long as you have leverage, you can play the game and play it well.* This is why it is a good strategy to get several offers simultaneously during the same time-period. Then, you can leverage one offer against the others. This is how you get your salary to move up, up, up.

> *As long as you have leverage, you can play the game and play it well.*

### Comparison Matrix

An attachment (not shown in this book) to the letter below shows a comparison matrix of three previous jobs vs. the current offers received. The person had negotiated the first two offers, but the hiring companies did not come up to the desired level, and, therefore, those offers were rejected. The job seeker could afford to reject them at the time.

## Strategy Used

Here is the strategy used for negotiating this offer. It was done by documenting the counter-offer in an email, showing the areas with which there were issues, and asking for consideration for more money, benefits, and/or perks in each of six areas of consideration. The job seeker received almost what was desired in items 1 and 2 and received all of items 4 and 5. However, nothing was received for items 3 and 6.

## Don't Leave Anything on the Table

If the job seeker had accepted the first offer without any negotiations, he would not have received the increase in salary plus the other benefits. If you do not ask, you will not receive. Additionally, you are worth only what you accept. Hence, *if you honestly feel you deserve more, then ASK!*

> *If you honestly feel you deserve more, then ASK!*

---

Dear Ms. Smith:

Thank you very much for the good offer that I have received from ABC Corporation (ABCC).

For your review, I have prepared/attached an Offer Comparison Matrix of the last three positions that I held at BX Software, Inc., Telecom, Inc., and The XYZ Corporation, respectively. I also included the recent offers that I had received from WWB Corporation and Vision Corporation.

Thank you for allowing me the time to evaluate your offer against offers from my past three jobs and other current opportunities. Before I accept the ABCC offer, I would appreciate it greatly if some consideration could be made either to exceed or equal my other career alternative opportunities. For example, I would appreciate it greatly if the following considerations could be made:

1. ***Base Salary***—Provide a base salary of $115K per annum. This amount is what my most recent employer (Vision Corporation) had paid me prior to my departure. I have had a six-figure annual income for the past eight consecutive years that ranged between $108K and $170K per year. Last year, I exceeded $130K from my employment at Vision Corporation.

2. ***Relocation Package***—Provide a relocation package (effective up to 18 months) to move from Marin County to somewhere in Riverside County. BX Software had offered me $25K to move from San Bernardino County to

Marin County in 1995 (nine years ago). Telecom, Inc., paid actual moving expenses that came to $25K including gross up. Additionally, Telecom paid me relocation bonuses totaling $35K (which included a $16K reimbursement of real estate fees including gross up). WWB Corporation had offered a $25K relocation package plus 30 days of temporary housing.

3. *Travel Expenses*—Provide reimbursement of travel expenses for six months. BX Software provided me with an expense-free use of a leased automobile for the duration of my employment with them. Telecom provided me with reimbursement of all expenses to operate a leased automobile for six months.

4. *Wireless Phone*—Provide a company paid wireless phone and pay for all calling expenses. The phone is necessary for me to perform my job effectively and to communicate with my wife at home during the long hours that I will be working in the evenings and on weekends (when required) during major proposal efforts. Both Telecom and XYZ Corporation provided me with this needed equipment. WWB was going to do likewise.

5. *Professional Dues*—Company payment of professional, annual, organizational dues, which shall not exceed a total of $500/year. BX Software, Telecom, Inc., and XYZ Corporation paid for these professional expenses. WWB Corporation was going to do likewise.

6. *Bonus Plan*—Provide some sort of bonus plan. I had bonus plans at BX Software, Telecom, and XYZ Corporation. Vision Corporation offered to provide me with an incentive bonus plan with no cap.

These requests do not even take into consideration stock options, which we had received from both Telecom and XYZ Corporation. It also does not consider a sign-on bonus that we had received from Telecom.

If serious consideration could be given to these requested adjustments, then I would start at ABC Corporation on a positive, enthusiastic note. I thank you in advance for any consideration that can be made to effect and facilitate my coming to ABCC. I await and anticipate your response.

If you desire to discuss this response by phone, I will be pleased to do so at your convenience. Thank you.

Sincerely yours,

John Doe

## *Negotiations*

Regarding negotiating, make sure you do sufficient research to ascertain the ranges of what the average salaries are for people doing the same or similar jobs in the locale where you would be working. If you have an outstanding resume, background, and skills to offer, you will have more leverage than if you are an average graduate.

### Approaches to Negotiating

If you have a lot of value to add to the company pursuing you, ask for the top or beyond the salary range prevailing for that locale. If you have only an average value to offer the company, you would probably be lucky to receive the midpoint of the salary range for that locale. And if they will not give you more salary, ask for perks or other benefits.

### Negotiation Examples

Here are three negotiations that I had with three companies, which gave me offers:

Company A adjusted the following:
- Came up on the salary from $93K to $96K per annum
- Increased my relocation from $20K to $25K
- Cell phone paid totally (all expenses) by the company
- Payment of my professional dues up to $500 each year

I turned them down.

Company B adjusted the following:
- Increased salary from $75K to $80K per annum
- Increased relocation from $5K to $10K
- Temporary housing up to 45 days
- Two expense paid trips for my wife to come and find a home
- No-cap bonus plan based on a percentage of all new business booked

I turned down their offer also.

Company C adjusted the following:
- Increased salary from $90K to $105K per annum
- Increased relocation to pay all expenses

- Cell phone with all expenses paid for by the company
- Professional dues paid up to $500 per year
- Computer in my home

I accepted this increased offer.

## Everything is Negotiable

Remember, *everything is negotiable*. However, if you do not ask, you will not receive anything more. So, ask!

> **Remember,**
> **everything**
> **is**
> **negotiable.**

## Negotiating a Good Salary Offer

*When negotiating an offer after an interview, you state that you should never accept the first offer presented. So, in an entry-level business position, what is fair to ask for? Of course, it will depend on the company, position, and applicant's qualifications, but can we get some case examples such as a college graduate with non-relevant job experience, a GPA of just over 3.0, and an offer of $41,000…? What could the applicant reasonably counter with?*

Job Seeker

### You Must Have Leverage to Negotiate from a Position of Strength

Yes, your negotiation ability and leverage depends on the company, position, and applicant's qualifications. If the prior jobs that a college graduate had included working in fast-food restaurants, digging ditches, cleaning out houses, and washing dishes, that person has not developed much leverage to command a greater salary or benefits upon receiving a job offer.

### Determine the Prevailing Benchmark Salary Ranges

The first thing any college student nearing graduation should do is to go on the Internet to find out the average salary ranges for the jobs being sought and in what city. From that, the job seeker could match what the going industry range is and what he/she needs and wants. What the job seeker needs should be the low number of his/her personal range and what he/she wants should be the high number of the personal range. Your acceptable amount should be the mid-range number.

## Conduct a Comparative Analysis

Now, this range should be compared to the range of salaries of those in the same jobs starting out in industry. If both ranges match up, then, great! If your personal need-want range is below the going industry range, you do not think much of your capabilities and probably have minimal leverage. If your personal need-want range is above the going industry range, you may have an over-inflated ego and probably do not have a good grasp of reality.

## SWEGs for CSUSM Graduates

Now, here are my scientific wide-eyed guesses (SWEGs) from what I have been hearing and seeing. If a CSUSM graduate receives between $35K and $45K per annum, she/he is doing well. If anyone receives below $30K per annum, she/he is not doing very well. *The average income poverty level for the continental United States is approximately $30K per year.* For Hawaii, it is $34K per year, and for Alaska, it is $37K per year. Hence, if you are making less than $30K per annum, you are living in poverty.

> ***The average income poverty level for the continental United States is approximately $30K per year.***

If anyone receives over $50K per annum, she/he is doing very well indeed. One or two students in each career development class should be able to obtain over $45K per annum. The next top five students in each career development class should be able to achieve between $40K–$45K per annum. The vast majority of the students in the class should be able to earn $35K–$40K per annum. A few students in the class may be able to earn between $30K–$35K per annum. Then, there may be one or two students who will not receive a job offer at all, and they will be living in poverty.

## National Averages

The national average salaries for newly minted B.S. degree holders in the fall of 2002 included the following:

| Analysis: National Average Salary for Fall 2002 (BS Degrees) | |
| --- | --- |
| **Degree Area** | **Annual Salary** |
| Software Design and Development | $53,524 |
| Computer Engineering | $51,135 |
| Electrical/Electronic Engineering | $50,391 |
| Computer Science | $49,413 |
| Mechanical Engineering | $48,282 |
| Construction Engineering | $43,794 |
| CEs/Project Engineering | $43,124 |
| Management Information Systems | $42,524 |
| Civil Engineering | $41,193 |
| Economics/Finance | $39,961 |
| English | $28,438 |
| Psychology | $26,738 |

### Averages for San Diego County

So, if I were to guess, the average salary range for graduates with BSBA degrees in San Diego County would be somewhere between $35K and $45K per annum. The average would be around $40K per annum, which would place it around the Economics/Finance job of $39,961 per annum. Of course, this is all debatable.

I would say that if you receive an offer of $41K per annum, you are doing well here in San Diego County. You would be making as much as a Civil Engineer. Notice that if you want to make good money, you should go into software, computers, and engineering. *People with soft degrees, such as English and Psychology, will most likely live in poverty.*

> *People with soft degrees, such as English and Psychology, will most likely live in poverty.*

### 2004 College Grads

Kate Lorenz wrote an article on "Salaries Are Increasing for New Grads," which was published on CareerBuilder.com. You might find this article beneficial. It supports what I said about BSBAs in the San Diego County area who should be paid between $35K-$45K/year. We see the following:

- Project Engineering $46,241
- Consulting $44,071
- Design or Construction Engineering $44,015
- Financial or Treasury Analysis $42,476
- Accounting (Public) $40,701
- Accounting (Private) $40,271
- Nursing $38,987
- Sales $35,118
- Management Trainee or Entry-Level Management $34,709/yr
- Teaching $29,266

Hence, there it is: $35K-$45K per year. If you receive $40K-$45K per year, you are doing very well indeed. As a sad note, however, the average teachers' salary indicates that they are living in poverty. Sad.

## Moving or Relocation Expenses

*What is a fair amount of relocation expenses that I should request if I do decide to take the offer? What should be included in the relocation expenses?*

Graduating Senior

The fair amount is anything you can get or whatever the traffic will bear. It all depends on the leverage you possess. Normally, top executives will get everything paid for including:

- Paid trips (including airfare, rental car, hotel, per diem, and other expenses) to the area with your spouse to go house hunting
- Payment of shipping all of your household goods
- Hotel rent for 30 days until you move into your new home
- Cost of selling of previous home
- Payment of closing costs and points
- Payment of any taxes
- Moving bonus
- Payment of any damages or loss of household goods during shipment

Sometimes, even managers, directors, and good engineers can receive some or most of these relocation expenses. Hence, you could receive anywhere from nothing to what are listed above. The bare minimum should be payment of rental truck for you to move your own household goods. I would try to get them to pay for the cost of a cross-country moving company to pack and move all of your household goods. However, again, it depends on how badly they want you.

Employees, with job freezes and payroll cuts fresh in their minds, may be reluctant to test their negotiating power. Of the employees surveyed by the Society for Human Resource Management and CareerJournal.com [in 2004], only 34% had attempted to negotiate their relocation costs, whereas 56% of the human-resource professionals interviewed said payments for relocation costs were negotiable.[10]

Still, your rank can make a difference. Says Joseph Morabito, president and chief executive officer of Paragon Global Resources Inc., a Rancho Santa Margarita, Calif., relocation company, "if it's a really high-level employee, then everything could be negotiable, everything could be on the table." For example, high-level executives might be reimbursed for the commission on selling a house, "a benefit that's usually not provided for lower-level employees."[11]

### You are Worth What You Accept

**Remember this maxim:** "*Whatever salary you accept is what you are worth*." Do not complain later on, particularly if another person with either the same or lesser qualifications ends up making more money than you.

For example, if you are an accountant, you will be privy to wage and salary rates of all of the employees in your company. It could get depressing if you found many people, who are not as good performers as you, making more money than you. However, if you subscribe to my maxim that "*you are worth what you accept*," then you should not feel bad at all if you found that you are one of the lower paid employees in the company. Learn, accept, and follow that principle.

> *Whatever salary you accept is what you are worth.*

---

10 Jennifer Lisle, "Relocation Benefits are Often Negotiable," taken from the CareerJournal.com, The Wall Street Journal Executive Career Site, located on http://www.careerjournal.com/salaryhiring/negotiate/20040527-lisle.html on 1/1/2006.

11 Ibid.

## *What People are Offered and Their Work Hours*

Here is a data point for you to consider. I know a person who graduated with a BS degree in accounting from a school of accountancy but received only $41K per year working for one of the big finance and accounting firms in the country. During tax season, he works from 8:00 AM to 10:00 PM every weekday as well on some Saturdays. They even expect him to work on Sundays, and he has done so. Being on salary, he does not receive any overtime pay.

## *Counteroffers*

### Be Prepared for Rejection

When making a counteroffer, be prepare for a "no" answer or worse, i.e., a total withdrawal of their offer. For me, that result does not bother me at all, so I can afford to take the risk of being bold but humble…and ultimately being rejected. However, I have never experienced rejection yet. Usually, the offering company wants me badly enough that they have always negotiated with me.

### Character Counts

Only you can decide as to what you should do. So, if the negotiation goes poorly, accept the result and do not blame someone else for your misfortune. That is a big part of one's character, i.e., to take full responsibility for the choices one makes instead of blaming everyone else except oneself. Character counts!

## *Negotiating Leverage of Recent College Graduates*

*What leverage does a college graduate have with no financial background? This is what is keeping me weary of negotiating too much.*

Recent Graduate

A college graduate does not have much leverage if he or she:

- Has not previously worked in the financial world (like a student working for his/her father who owns a financial business…these are the students who have a huge "leg up" on their peers)
- Does not have a finance or accounting degree but has a degree in some other field such as business administration

- Has not built up some experience working as an intern in a financial business and has not served in leadership positions in related financial professional organizations

## MBA Graduates Have More Leverage

As graduating business-school (B-School) students hit the job market, they may be in store for more opportunities and better pay than recent grads. A survey conducted by the Graduate Management Admission Council found that recruiter optimism about the economy is translating into more openings this year [2005]. Overall, the estimated starting salary for MBA graduates for 2005 is $78,040, up from $72,021 in 2001–2002. When benefits and perks are added, the overall compensation package for an MBA hire averages $96,657.[12]

Employers in a recent survey reported base starting salaries that ranged from a low of $34,000 to a high of $103,000. More than half plan to pay their new MBAs more than $75,000 a year. And more than half of the respondents, 58.3%, expect to "sweeten the pot" with a signing bonus.[13]

| Starting MBA Salary | % of Employers Offering |
| --- | --- |
| $50,000 or under | 14.9% |
| $50,001–$75,000 | 32.4 |
| $75,001–$100,000 | 51.4 |
| $100,001 or more | 1.4 |

## In Conclusion...

### Be Confident in Your Decisions

Well, these are my thoughts. Whatever you do, once you make a decision, press forward. Do not look backward. Look forward. Do not allow yourself to experience "buyer's remorse." Whether your decisions are right or wrong, be confident and proud of your decisions.

---

12 Lex Kaptik, "Negotiating Strategies for New MBA Grads," taken from *CareerJournal.com*, The Wall Street Journal Executive Career Site, at URL http://www.careerjournal.com/salaryhiring/negotiate/20050602-kaptik.html on 1/1/2006.

13 Ibid.

## Believe in Yourself

Do not regret whatever you decide to do and then things turn sour. Be decisive. Always believe in yourself. Always do what you believe to be right and stick with it. Do not be wishy-washy. Do not do what is politically correct. Follow your passion. Be a leader, not a follower. You have a great career before you.

*Chapter 5*

# Negotiating a Salary—Part 2

*When you are negotiating for your pay package, be sure to explain your reason for asking for specific things or amounts. It is not reasonable simply to say, "I want it." You should have a clear and convincing business reason for asking for something. Identify the reasons something is supportive of the business' agenda, or why it is clearly a competitive issue.*[14]

Bill Coleman
Senior Vice President of Compensation

### *Those Who Seek, Find; Those Who Ask, Receive*

I certainly like the spunk that some people possess. Most people would never come back to the well the second time. When you do and have a good point, I listen. When someone does that, this is what I usually do. I give them a chance to get something for their efforts. *Remember, there is always more than one way to skin a cat.*

> **Remember, there is always more than one way to skin a cat.**

I want more people to be like those few who will come back to the well when you feel that you have a case to plead. I don't know if it can be taught to people, but if you possess that gift, continue being that way throughout life. *The rewards usually go to the people who make the extra effort. Being assertive is not being difficult.*

> **The rewards usually go to the people who make the extra effort.**

---

14 Bill Coleman, SVP of Compensation, "When and How to Negotiate," *Salary.com*, extracted on 6/17/05.

There are always extenuating circumstances. Rules can be changed. Barriers can always be jumped over, crawled under, scooted around, or plowed through. There is always more than one answer to life's questions. Whatever the mind can conceive and believe can be achieved. *There is always a better way. Seek it out…always.*

> **Being assertive is not being difficult.**

## Negotiating Salary with No Work Experience

*I have heard that you should always negotiate your salary. In my situation, with no work experience, I feel I should take whatever offer I can in order to get work experience. I feel I will be worth more once I get more experience. Is it bad to take the first offer if it is at an industry average for an entry level position?*

### Always Try to Negotiate a Better Deal

Please understand that "negotiating your salary" does not imply that you will get a better deal in every situation. You can negotiate all you want and never get an increase or anything else. However, you will never know that unless and until you actually make an attempt to negotiate your salary, the offer you receive, or anything else. Hence, I always say, *"Everything is negotiable. You should never accept the first offer. Always try to negotiate a better deal."* So, do you understand what I am saying here?

> **Everything is negotiable. You should never accept the first offer. Always try to negotiate a better deal.**

### If You Ask, You are Negotiating

If you don't ask, nobody will ever throw any more money at you than what you expect. Hence, I also say, *"You are worth exactly what you accept, no more."* If you do not attempt to negotiate your offer, you will never know whether or not you left anything on the table. *What's the worst that could happen to you if you ask? They wouldn't kill you.* And if they withdraw the offer, you wouldn't want to work for a company with such a "take it or leave it" attitude anyway. So, ask! Just by asking, you are negotiating.

> **What's the worst that could happen to you if you ask? They wouldn't kill you.**

## When to Accept the First Offer

If you are hard up, don't know where your next meal is coming from, and don't ever want to risk losing the offer, then accept the first offer. However, if you have money in the bank and aren't hard up, negotiate, negotiate, negotiate!

## As a Man Thinketh

Yes, you will be worth more once you gain more experience. However, like I said before, if you don't think you are worth more right now, then you should go ahead and accept the first offer. You absolutely cannot receive more salary than you think you are worth right now. *As a man thinketh, so is he.* You are worth exactly what you think you're worth, and that's all you will accept, no more. If you think you are worth only what you are being offered, then accept the offer because that's all you are worth.

## Be Above the Industry Average

No, it is not bad to accept the first offer if it is at the industry average for an entry level position. However, if the offer is below the industry average, then it would be unwise to accept that offer. It may take you years to catch up to that industry average. And when you do, the industry average will have again risen. So, you will forever be behind the industry average curve unless you make a paradigm shift in your thinking and never accept anything below the industry average on your next job search. The ideal, of course, is to be above the industry average. To be that, however, you must be a "mover and a shaker."

> *Be a mover and a shaker.*

## How Do You Negotiate a Better Offer if Pay Scales are Pre-established?

*How would you negotiate an offer if the company bases salary on your experience and do not offer perks as you mentioned in class? I work for a college where the pay scale is already set up and depends on experience. Any suggestions especially if you feel that you can do the job that is available but don't have the experience.*

Senior Student

## Life is Too Short to Work for Inflexible Organizations

I don't know of any company or establishment that you cannot negotiate anything. Yes, some governmental organizations have set pay scales. However, there are many kinds of perquisites (perks) that can be negotiated. If they give you absolutely no room for salary or perks negotiations, then, perhaps, you should find an organization that provides you with some room for negotiations. There are too many good organizations out there that you do not need to be forced to limit yourself only to just one…the one that will not negotiate anything. Life is too short for that.

### Develop Your Own Leverage

If you have no experience in the job you want to get into, then you need to take preparatory jobs that will give you that experience. You can also get an advanced degree and specialize in that new career area. Furthermore, you can complete a certification program in that new job area.

### Prepare Yourself for What You Desire

Join professional organizations in the career field you seek to enter. Participate in the local chapter of these organizations. More than one way exists to acquire the education and experience needed to get into your passion job. You need to find those ways to prepare yourself for what you desire.

## How to Negotiate a Good Salary

*How does the interviewee go about negotiating salaries with an employer?*

Struggling Student

### Leverage is Power

First, *to be able to negotiate a good salary with an employer, you must have leverage.* Leverage is the power to maximize the offer including salary, bonuses, stock options, moving of household goods, benefits, perquisites, and other advantages. If you possess no leverage, you may be forced to take whatever is offered, or you may attempt to negotiate at your own peril.

> *To be able to negotiate a good salary with an employer, you must have leverage.*

## What Constitutes Leverage?

You have leveraging power if you possess:

- A current, good job with a company that thinks highly of you
- An outstanding resume that "packs a punch"
- An excellent employment background and track record
- Extensive experience to offer what the company is seeking
- Advanced degrees
- An impressive job interview
- A lot of money in the bank so you don't need to worry if you get a job or not
- Several simultaneous offers from companies that are hotly pursuing you

If you possess all of these strengths, you have tremendous leveraging power. In that case, you can negotiate to the hilt and squeeze out the best salary possible.

## Tactical vs. Strategic Approach to Work

*Is it worth taking a pay cut in order to obtain a higher level in a company? For example: A bellman at the Four Seasons hotel can make a lot of money in tips. In total, they can make more money than an assistant manager on salary. Is it worth giving up the tip benefits to advance further in the company through obtaining an assistant manager position?*

An Employee

### Be Strategically Oriented

Yes, it is worth taking a pay cut in order to obtain a higher level in a company. Too many people now-a-days don't look any further than the end of their noses. They are so tactically oriented instead of strategically oriented that they would rather get lots of money now rather than to put it off for much more money later on. People would rather be cocktail waitresses, bartenders, and bellmen (going for the tips) and taking a promotion for a job that they do not like or would not want to make a career of instead of laying a firm foundation for a career field that they could be passionate about.

## Instant Gratification

Many people want instant gratification. They do not want to pay their dues. They would rather start at president and then work their way down rather than start as a trainee and work their way up to president. That's the way it is these days. People want everything but they won't spend the time and sacrifice necessary to build a firm foundation before building up the rest of the house. That's why, more often than not, they soon come crashing down in defeat and failure.

## Pay Your Dues

I remember working at Hamilton Standard Division of United Technologies Corporation where the vice president of the Space Systems Division started his career 30 years earlier as the guard at the front door. He worked to obtain his education including advanced degrees and slowly but surely worked his way up the ladder until he was in charge of an important division of the company. That's the way it should be done. He paid his dues all along the way. *Everyone should pay his or her dues.*

> *Everyone should pay his or her dues.*

## When to Discuss Salary or Compensation

*At what point of an interview and which interview, whether it is in the first or tenth interview, is it appropriate to discuss salary or compensation issues?*

College Senior

## Never Bring Up Salary First

Whatever number interview it is, *do not discuss salary unless and until the interviewer brings it up.* Sometimes, during the first interview, the interviewer asks, "How much in annual salary are you expecting?" Now, this is a dangerous question at this point, particularly if he/she asks you this question early in the first interview. Chances are the interviewer is only attempting to determine whether he/she wants to eliminate you from further consideration.

> *Do not discuss salary unless and until the interviewer brings it up.*

### Stare Your Interviewer Straight in the Eyes

So, how do you respond? With a question like what the interviewer asked, you respond with another question, "Are you making me an offer?" Then, stare him/her in the eyes. This is where you find out if the interviewer is serious enough or not about wanting you to fill the vacancy. The interviewer's answer, at this point, will be very revealing as to whether or not he/she is really interested in you to hire or whether he/she is just trying to eliminate you from further consideration.

### Keep the Interviewer On the Defensive

If the interviewer says that he/she is not making you an offer at that time, then, in a very nice way, respond with, "When you are ready to make me an offer, I'll be able to let you know how much I am expecting." If the interviewer insists and keeps coming back at you, respond with another question, "What is the salary range for this position?" If the interviewer says he/she can't give you that information, then, respond with, "When you can give me a range of the available salary, then I'll tell you what salary I am expecting." *Always keep the interviewer on the defensive, but do it in a nice, friendly manner.*

> *Always keep the interviewer on the defensive, but do it in a nice, friendly manner.*

### Finding a Reason to Eliminate You

All the interviewer is trying to do is to find a reason to eliminate you. That's the name of the game. If the interviewer doesn't like your assertiveness, then you don't want to work for a person or company who wants you to play only by their rules. That's how you become an indentured servant.

### Wait for an Offer

Ms. Valerie Patterson, senior producer for CareerJournal.com in South Brunswick, New Jersey, said, "Ironically, in the early stage of negotiating compensation, the important thing isn't what you say, but what you don't say: You absolutely do not want to discuss money unless an offer is on the table."[15] So, as I said earlier, never bring up salary first.

---

15 Valerie Patterson, "Earning the Salary You Want in Today's Tough Economy," *The Wall Street Journal Online*, CareerJournal.com, March 30, 2004.

## Take Charge of Your Own Career

If the interviewer eliminates you because of your assertive responses, at least he/she won't have your expected salary figure to add to the company's salary statistics. That is one way that companies find out what the going rate is for similar jobs in their industry. This is why you should never include your expected salary in your cover letter or resume. Don't give them data to figure out industry salaries without getting anything for it. *Be in charge of your own career.*

> *Be in charge of your own career.*

## Negotiating a Higher Starting Salary

*Someone had mentioned that the reason she got the large increase in salary when she accepted the job was because she asked for it and that she had a tool to figure out what she was worth. I am having a really difficult time at my job, being unhappy in general, and I want to seriously look for a new position while I am working on my application for a federal agency. I would like to be able to negotiate a higher starting salary with whatever company, but I am not sure as to how to go about it. Any help would be greatly appreciated. By the way, do you know any local companies that are hiring right now?*

Unhappy Employee

## This Too Will Pass

You may be having a really difficult time at your job and being unhappy in general, but keep it internal and not let your unhappiness appear on the surface. This too will pass. Make the best of what you have until you can get a better job. In the meantime, keep working hard on trying to capture that better, new job.

## Positive Mental Attitude and Supreme Confidence

*The most important thing about negotiating a higher starting salary is to start with a positive mental attitude.* You must believe that you are worth more than what you are currently being paid before you ever will convince anyone with the gold to pay you a dollar more. You must have supreme confidence in yourself and your worth even if it means walking away from a pot of gold just because they didn't have enough dollars in

> *The most important thing about negotiating a higher starting salary is to start with a positive mental attitude.*

the pot. And you must be able to walk away without feeling bad at all! Can you do that? Only if you can do that will you ever receive more money than you are worth.

## Prove Your Worth

At any rate, you are not worth any more than what you are willing to accept. Or in other words, you are only worth what you are willing to accept. If you accept less than what the personal worth tool computes on you, that's all you are worth. If you accept more than what the personal worth tool computes on you, that's what you're worth. *The trick is that you must convince the person with the gold that you are worth every penny he/she pays you.* Then, once they pay you a certain salary, you must prove on the job that you are worth every cent of that salary.

> *The trick is that you must convince the person with the gold that you are worth every penny he/she pays you.*

## The Best Jobs to Pursue

If I wanted to identify local companies that are hiring, I would get a list of the companies in the area that I would like to work for and then go to their websites to see what openings they currently have available. Also, if you can find someone you know who currently works in that company, you may be able to find out about job openings that haven't yet been posted on their website. These are the best jobs to pursue.

## Negotiating a Salary

*How do you negotiate your salary?*

A Job Neophyte

### Always Negotiate From a Position of Strength

Very carefully! I seriously really mean that. Do not rush any salary negotiation. Take your sweet time. The longer you take, the better off you'll be. If you don't have much leverage, you will not be very successful. *If you possess a lot of leverage, you can negotiate things to the hilt.* So, take your time, and always negotiate from a position of strength.

> *If you possess a lot of leverage, you can negotiate things to the hilt.*

## Get Your Ducks Lined Up

Do not negotiate over the phone unless you must do it that way. You want to see the whites of the hiring manager's eyeballs. Document your counteroffer in a letter. Give the hiring company time to evaluate your counteroffer. Suggest a date/time to come to the plant to discuss the matter. Gather all necessary data/information and be prepared for a face-to-face negotiating session.

## Ask In a Humble Way

*Always ask for more salary and other benefits in a humble, requesting way.* Don't be demanding. You must ask if you ever want to receive anything more than what they offer you. So, ask and ye shall receive.

> *Always ask for more salary and other benefits in a humble, requesting way.*

## Leverage in Negotiating Your Salary

*How much influence or validity does the interviewee have when it comes to negotiating salary, granted that the person is completely qualified for all of the aspects of the position? In other words, how much room for negotiating is allowed?*

Student

## Four Rules for Negotiating Salary

The interviewee has all of the influence he/she wants and needs and all the influence he/she can muster. After all, you determine what you want, and you determine what you will accept. There are four rules for negotiating salary:

- Everything is negotiable
- Ask and ye shall receive (If you don't ask, you won't get)
- You are worth exactly what you accept, no more
- Expect the best and get it

## You are Empowered

You are allowed all the room for negotiating that you desire. You are empowered to get the best salary you feel you deserve. Only you set the limits. If you think you are worth only $40K/year and accept that amount, but the hiring manager was prepared to give you $45K/year, then all you're worth is $40K/year, not

$45K/year. That's it! *Don't be unhappy if you accept less than what the hiring manager is prepared to give you.*

> **Don't be unhappy if you accept less than what the hiring manager is prepared to give you.**

## Maximize Your Leverage

You maximize what you get in negotiations by doing the following to maximize your leverage so that you can negotiate from a position of strength:

- Know what you're worth
- Know what people of your age, experience, and caliber make annually in your industry
- Be confident in yourself (Don't look and act hard-up)
- Demand what you want (in a nice way, of course)
- Build a dynamite of a track record
- Prepare a great resume with bullets that "pack a punch"
- Interview successfully and ask the right three questions to know you will receive an offer
- Get several offers simultaneously (in writing)
- Go slowly and methodically (never rush the negotiating process)
- Use your strengths in negotiating the best salary and benefits you can get
- Leave nothing on the table during negotiations
- Be prepared for rejection and losing the offer (So what if they withdraw the offer?)

## *Discussions on Salary Not Geared to College Graduates?*

*You said we should make note to argue about things you say that we don't agree with, so here I go. I was telling someone about Heather Manley and how she got the $15,000 extra she asked for. They said they knew all about the situation and that David Bennett was her mentor, and he had something to do with her getting that raise. They would not have done it for just anyone.*

*I am not saying that this comment must be true, but it makes you think. The whole thing about not accepting offers for less than what you're worth is good info, but the way you talk about it, again doesn't really apply to us. We are fresh into the job market, and need to get as much experience as we can now. I just think that this discussion, well these discussions, is not really geared towards us. That's all.*

### Develop Your Leverage

Remember, these discussions aren't only for soon-to-be college graduates but are also for you to keep in your memory bank for use in future years. Like I said, if you don't know where your next meal is coming from, you may be forced to take whatever is offered to you. But for those who have a fantastic track record (and we usually have a couple in every class), a lot to offer, sufficient money in the bank, and if they are in great demand, then they have what's called leverage.

### Believe and Know That You Do Have Leverage

*If you have leverage, you can negotiate a job offer to the hilt. However, if you don't have leverage, then you must take whatever you can get.* The first requirement for possessing leverage is to believe and know that you do have leverage. If you don't believe you have leverage at the get-go, then you have no negotiating power and should probably accept whatever you are offered.

> **If you have leverage, you can negotiate a job offer to the hilt. However, if you don't, then you must take whatever you can get.**

### Develop a Track Record

College MBA graduates from the top business schools in the U.S. get top offers (for many them, over $100K/annum) with only three years of business experience! But, if you look at their track records, they can just about "walk on water." They have a lot of leverage, and they know it. Hence, they get what they demand and deserve.

### Blaine T. Murakami

As an example of someone who "walks on water," the May 16, 2005, *UH News* announced that Blaine T. Murakami, an engineering student who graduated this past semester from the University of Hawai'i at Manoa, was named the winner of the 2005 Alton B. Zerby and Carl T. Koerner Outstanding Electrical and Computer Engineering Student Award. The award, which was presented by the national electrical engineering society, Eta Kappa Nu, recognizes the most out-standing electrical engineering student in the United States.

### Outstanding Electrical Engineering Student in the US

Murakami is the third UH Manoa student to win the award in the past five years. Previous UH Manoa awardees are Kendall Ching (2001) and Aaron Ohta (2003).

Murakami has a long list of achievements as a UH Manoa undergraduate. For example, he:

- Co-authored one book chapter and 13 conference papers
- Is co-inventor on a pending patent
- Co-wrote a research proposal that captured a $100,000 award
- Led a multidisciplinary team of 30 electrical and mechanical engineering undergraduate students to design, build, and test two nano-satellites for launch into low-Earth orbit (LEO)

As a junior, Murakami:

- Co-founded a local high-technology company, Pipeline Communications and Technology, Inc.
- The company's business plan took first place in the 2004 UH Business Plan Competition
- The company recently won a contract of over $250,000 to develop the self-steering antenna technology of which Murakami is a co-inventor

Murakami's other awards include the following:

- UH Regents Scholarship
- 2005 Student Engineer of the Year Award from the Hawai'i Society of Professional Engineers
- Hawai'i Space Grant Consortium Undergraduate Fellowship
- IEEE Microwave Theory and Techniques Society Scholarship
- IEEE Antennas and Propagation Society Scholarship[16]

---

16 Contact: Wayne Shiroma, "UH Manoa graduate is nation's top electrical engineering student," *UH News*, University of Hawaii at Manoa, Posted: May 16, 2005, http://www.hawaii.edu/cgi-bin/uhnews?20050516144510.

### Work to Become "World Class" in Your Area of Expertise

Now, after reading this guy's track record in college, can you understand that he has a tremendous amount of leverage when he negotiates a job offer? I'll assure you, he will get just about anything he asks for. That's the kind of leveraged position you can maneuver yourself into if you work to become "world class" in your area of expertise.

### You Must Believe In Yourself

Of all the students in our class, my perception of you is that you have the track record and ability to wield a lot of leverage in everything you do. However, if you, personally, don't believe that, then you won't achieve whatever your potential would allow you to obtain.

### Value is a Figment of the Imagination

Much of value is a figment of the imagination…both the hiring manager's imagination and your imagination. If both you and the hiring manager imagine you to be "world class" and worth $100K per year, then that salary could be realized. However, if one of the parties don't really believe that, then you will never receive what would be considered a great offer.

### Power Brokers

Part of networking is to network with the right people who can and will make things happen for you. If you do not work to be "in" with these power brokers, then no matter how smart you are or how hard you work, you will not achieve these benefits. So, learn from it. Don't try to figure out why it can't work, won't work, or that it was only a unique situation. If you can figure out what people do to get the gold, learn from them, apply their strategies and tactics to your career, and you too can accomplish what they do.

### Perception is Everything

I may mentally have you up on a pedestal. Only you can change that mental image that I have of you. It is the same for all your peers. If I help build your image up in their minds and they believe it, then, to them, you are way up there on the totem pole. However, if you don't believe it, then by your attitudes, actions, and body language, you will change their perception of you, and you will come sliding down their mental totem pole. *Everything is relative. Perception counts for a lot. You* can accomplish anything if you think you can. Whatever the mind can conceive and believe can be achieved.

> *Everything is relative. Perception counts for a lot. You can accomplish anything if you think you can.*

### Self-fulfilling Prophecy

If you will go throughout your career believing all that I preach to you does not apply to you. Twenty years from now, you will still believe that those things I said will not apply to you even though you may be almost 45 years old. A self-fulfilling prophesy will be in full swing here.

### Paradigm Shift

Every accomplishment starts from the mind. If you cannot make that paradigm shift, then there is nothing I can do for you on that count. Only you can make happen whatever happens in your career. I can only give you some ideas, food for thought, motivation, and strategies/tactics. However, for anything positive to happen, only each person can make things happen in his/her life.

### Take It or Leave It

You can take or leave what I say, but remember what I said after about 20 years from now to see if you have achieved significant things without practicing the principles I have been teaching you.

## Expect the Best and Get It!

*I will expect the best, but I am always afraid that I am expecting too much. I do not know how to measure what I am worth. I am after all just graduating. I do not know how picky I can be at this point in my career.*

### Expect the Best with Confidence

To get the best, you must expect the best, i.e., expect the best and get it. Expecting the best and being afraid are incompatible. You must expect the best with confidence. If you are afraid, then you are not confident.

### Negotiate with Confidence

Linda Matias said, "When you are negotiating your wages, you need to be confident in your answers, and in what you are asking. If the question never comes up during the interview, then you need to initiate the topic. Look the employer in the eye, showing you are not afraid of any topic, any time. Ask what the salary is. If the answer is not high enough for you, add additional questions."[17]

## What You Expect is What You're Worth

You measure your worth by where you place the value line for yourself. If you think you are worth $30K/year, then that's exactly what you're worth because that's what you'll accept. If you think you are worth $50K/year, then that's exactly what you're worth, providing that's what you will accept...nothing less.

## Hard Concept to Follow

One needs to walk away from a deal if one doesn't get what he/she wants. That's how you make people know that you are worth what you really believe you are worth. *You must be willing to walk away if people don't meet your expectations.* That's a hard concept (pill) for many people to swallow. Now, whenever you make a decision (as painful as it may sometimes be) and do walk away, don't allow yourself to entertain "buyer's remorse" and don't look back. Forge ahead onward and upward!

> *You must be willing to walk away if people don't meet your expectations.*

## Thinking Must Be Congruent with Accepting

So, my maxim states: *You are worth exactly what you accept.* What you think you are worth and what you accept must be congruent. Hence, people keep lowering what they will accept until it coincides with what they think they are worth. Hence, that's what they are worth. Do you understand that logic?

> *You are worth exactly what you accept.*

## Elite of the World

You say, "I am after all just graduating." What do you mean, you are just graduating! Ninety percent of the people of the world don't graduate from college much less high school. Ninety-five percent don't get a master's degree. Only less

---

17  Linda Matias, "How to Negotiate the Perfect Salary," extracted on 5/23/2006 from net-temps.com, Net-Temps, Inc.

than one percent gets a doctorate degree. By being a college graduate, you are one of the elite of the world. What do you mean, "I am after all just graduating"!

### Atti Rattanatray

You do not know how picky you can be at this point in your career? You can be as picky as you want to be. You can go through life taking whatever comes your way, or you can go out and choose whatever you want. Nobody holds you back except you, yourself. You can have anything you desire if you want it bad enough. Self doubt is the anti-Christ of accomplishing great things. This is a take-off from what Atti Rattanatray has as his personal brand statement (PBS), i.e., *"Procrastination is the anti-Christ of production and progression."*

> *"Procrastination is the anti-Christ of production and progression."*
> **Atti Rattanatray**

### Expect the Best

So, *expect the best and get it. You will only get what you expect…no more.* If you do not expect the best, you will not get the best. No great thing ever occurs without heightened expectations.

> *Expect the best and get it. You will only get what you expect…no more.*

## Chapter 6
# Negotiating Promotions

---

**FACT:** *The biggest raises come from salary negotiations when choosing to move on to a NEW employer. Internal raises rarely exceed 5–8% but major increases—20%, 40%, even 50%,—come from selling yourself more effectively to a new company. New employers are offering top dollar just to insure you'll join their team, but ONLY if you know the secrets of salary negotiations. So if your employer isn't paying the true value of what you provide working for them, now is a good time to explore landing a new job with a much higher salary. But avoid committing salary negotiations suicide—do not break this rule: Never reveal your previous salary. Do learn how to effectively sell yourself and know your worth.*[18]

Robin Ryan
Career Counselor

## Asking for a Promotion

*Once hired, when can you ask for your first promotion? Is there a time rule? If there is a time rule, how does this change if you negotiated a higher salary when you first accepted your job? I hear about people receiving one, three, or five promotions in one year. How did these people know it was time to ask for another promotion?*

---

18 Robin Ryan, "Want a Raise? Don't Commit Salary Suicide," Net-Temps, Inc., Copyright 1995–2006, http://www.net-temps.com/careerdev/crossroads/print.htm?id=1771. America's most popular career counselor, Robin Ryan, is the author of four best-selling books. Contact her at 425-226-0414; email: info@robinryan.com.

## No Time Rule for Asking for a Promotion

There is no time rule for asking for a promotion. Asking for a promotion is like asking for a raise. If you have no leverage, don't bother or risk getting laughed out of your supervisor's office. You can ask for a promotion at any time; however, if you want to be successful at it, you must have accomplished great and wonderful things for your company. Just doing your job description, duties, and responsibilities does not warrant receiving a promotion or raise.

## How to Get Multiple Promotions in a Year

Getting a promotion and/or a raise has nothing to do with what salary you currently have (whether it is high or low). To receive three or five promotions in a year, you must:

- Have accomplished phenomenal things,
- Be in the "family," or
- Be the best buddy of the person with the gold (purse strings).

## Walking On Water

*If you figuratively "walk on water," you don't need to ask for promotions.* Management will be looking out for your welfare and promoting you on a sufficiently accelerated schedule to keep your expertise and abilities within the company. So, just generate some earthshaking inventions and acquire patents on them. Those achievements will increase your "value" to the company. Hence, top management will be looking out for your welfare and promoting you rapidly. If you become a Nobel Prize winner, management will automatically do whatever it takes to keep you within the corporation.

> *If you figuratively "walk on water," you don't need to ask for promotions.*

## How Not to Get Promoted

*If you work only eight hours a day, don't expect a promotion.* If you will not do anything but your job description, do not expect a promotion. If you want a balanced life, do not expect a promotion. If you will not travel incessantly for the company, do not expect a promotion. If you will not put in long, unpaid

> *If you work only eight hours a day, don't expect a promotion.*

hours, do not expect a promotion. If you are not creative, innovative, and add value, do not expect a promotion.

## The "You Owe Me" Society

The trouble with most greedy people today is that they don't do anything of significance, yet they expect promotions and raises. That's the "you owe me" society we have transitioned into over the past half century. Nobody is owed anything unless they are truly the "movers and shakers" in the company. *Those who do "diddly-squat" always seem to* **expect** *the world from their company.* If you personally double the size of the company, say from $10 million to $20 million of revenue in one year, then you deserve a promotion, and everybody will know it.

> *Those who do "diddly-squat" always seem to expect the world from their company.*

## *Talking to Your Boss about Job Promotions*

*Say I have been working at a company for six months where I am bored with my position and want to be promoted to a position where I can be challenged more, and as a result, I can benefit the company more. Do I stay in the position and find ways to improve myself and the company, or do I approach my boss and share with him my desire?*

### Stay in a Job for at Least a Year

Since you have been at your present company for six months, looking for new work at another company should be out of the question. You should be in a job for a minimum of at least one year. So, you shouldn't even try to transfer to another job within the same company. What you are left to do are as you suggested:

- Stay in the position and look for ways to improve yourself and the company
- Approach your boss and share with him your desire to be promoted to a position where you can be challenged more

### Display Initiative

Bullet number one is your best bet. Seek out ways to improve yourself by taking courses, volunteering to do other tasks not in your job description, and look for ways to improve company processes, procedures, and systems. Here is your chance to display your initiative. Here is a chance for you to be creative and innovative. Here is your chance to make a difference, add value, and make things happen.

## Talk to Your Boss

Bullet number two is good only if your boss will actually give you a bona fide promotion, which is a long shot indeed. After all, you've been on the job for only six months. You should not take a lateral transfer. It would not look good on your resume to have a job for only six months. However, if you are actually promoted to a higher, better position, then it won't look bad on your resume. In fact, it would look good on your resume.

## No Time for Boredom—Do Something

At any rate, don't just sit there and be bored for another day. Challenge yourself to be proactive and seek things to do that would force you to grow. This is how you could get promoted. Your boss won't promote a bored direct report. However, if you start doing something significant, that would spark him on to promote you perhaps by the time you are with the company for a year. That would be the best time to promote you anyway. So, don't waste the next six months by being bored. *Get up and do something. Make things happen. Be a mover and shaker. Help the company grow and progress.* If you did all of that stated above, you wouldn't have time to be bored.

> *Get up and do something. Make things happen. Be a mover and shaker. Help the company grow and progress.*

## Asking Your Boss about Job Promotions

*Is it okay to ask a boss directly about promotions (process and possibilities) or is there another way to find out about this information?*

## Get Your Supervisor to Like You

Yes, this is the best way to go about getting promoted. If you ever want to get promoted, you need to let your boss know that you are interested in being promoted for good work. So, ask your boss/supervisor about the promotion process and possibilities. Generally, you will never get promoted if it is not first initiated by your immediate supervisor. So, it is extremely important that your supervisor likes you. I don't know of any supervisors who promoted anyone he/she did not like.

## Ask Your Supervisor

Sometimes there may be a company policy and/or procedure regarding promotions. You could obtain a copy of them and review them to understand the promotion process, criteria for promoting someone, and other information regarding promotions. But the best way to find out about these things is to ask your supervisor. This lets your supervisor know that you are interested in being promoted for good work in the future.

## Promotion or Career Path Fit?

*My boss just recently offered me a higher position within the company. With this promotion, I would obtain a more prestigious title and higher pay. Unfortunately, I am not currently in the industry that I would like to pursue a career in. I'm apprehensive towards this promotion because I don't want to lose out on other opportunities that would better suit my career path. Should I accept the position or find another one that better fits my career path?*

### Analyze Your Alternatives

Okay, here are your alternatives. You can accept the position, or you can decline the promotion and then start looking for a new job. If you accept the position, you would receive more money and prestige. However, you could get type-set into that career field because you are now in management. You could get "locked in" and later find it extremely difficult to change industries and jobs. If you were successful in making the change, in most likelihood, you would need to take a reduction in pay to start anew in a different job and new industry.

### Seek Work You Would Enjoy Doing

*We should try as best as possible to find work in a position and industry that fits our passion, desires, capabilities, talents, interests, and typology.* In that way, we would enjoy our work more. Because we would be enjoying our work more, we would tend to do better on the job. If we do better, we are more prone to be very successful at it. And when we are successful at it, we will receive the many benefits associated with success.

> **We should try as best as possible to find work in a position and industry that fits our passion, desires, capabilities, talents, interests, and typology.**

### Plan Your Career Path

Additionally, it would be better to plan your career path such that you possess increasing, relevant jobs in the same area of your passion. Your resume would look better. You will create a better image in the minds of those reviewing your resume. And you will gain experience that will facilitate reaching your goals in your career and life.

### Short-run vs. Long-run

On the other hand, like someone who takes a job as a cocktail waitress or bartender because the current pay is better, in the long run, that job may be detrimental to one's career in a totally different field. Additionally, the added prestige of a higher position and more money because of a promotion in a field you are not excited about, you will benefit more in the short run but would perhaps lose in the long run.

### Sacrifice Now for Future Benefits

I know fellow high school graduates who were now-oriented, so they forwent college and took jobs as laborers in the construction industry. They made pretty good money relative to us starving college students. However, once the students graduated from college and acquired good salaried jobs, it wasn't long before they passed their fellow high school alumni in pay and prestige because they forwent the immediate high wage of construction work for the future earnings of a college graduate.

### Tactically or Strategically Oriented?

It depends on whether you are tactically oriented or strategically oriented. Those who are tactically oriented look for the big bucks and big titles that would help them right now. However, those who are strategically oriented look for developing a career background and path that may not provide them with as much money or prestige now but, in all likelihood, would propel them to greater heights in the long run. So, are you short-range oriented or long-range oriented? That's the difference.

## Asking for Special Attention and Promotions

*After I start working at my new job for a year or two years, should I directly ask my manager for more responsibilities to get more attention, appreciation, and raises? I don't know if it's a good idea to do because I notice that other co-workers who have been there longer do not get any promotion or special attention.*

### Seek More Responsibility

You should ask your manager for more responsibilities when you first start working at your new job, not a year or two after you start. Show your supervisor that you are always willing to learn more and to take on new duties and responsibilities. Go to him/her periodically during your down times and offer your assistance and help in doing things that you have not done before.

### Display Initiative and Willingness

Show him/her your initiative and willingness to do more. If you do these things and do a good job at all of your assigned action items, tasks, and projects, you will receive more attention, appreciation, and raises.

### Problem Employees or Problem Management?

If your co-workers have been there longer than one or two years but have not yet received any promotions or special attention, the question is begged: Did they periodically go to the manager to offer help and seek out more responsibilities? If not, you know why they have not received any promotions or special attention. If they have done those things, then perhaps it is a systemic problem where recognition, promotions, and raises are not given out often enough to keep the employees motivated and working hard.

### A Systemic Problem?

If it is a systemic problem, you have two alternatives to change things: (1) use your initiative and try to get the company to improve in these areas or (2) seek work in another better company that have an active program for giving attention, showing appreciation, giving frequent promotions and raises, and giving special attention to productive employees. So, be a mover and shaker and make things happen in your company. If you do that, you will receive deserved recognition, promotions, and raises.

## Is Sucking Up to the Boss a Good Strategy?

*In my work experience, it seems that those who "suck up" to the boss the most seem to be the ones who get all the promotions, etc., regardless of their work ability. In your opinion, do you think that the best way to get ahead in your career is to suck up and get in good with the boss also, or do you think that your skills and hard work matter more, or could it be a combination of the two?*

### Paradigm Shift Needed

You need a paradigm shift. You are seeing your glass as half empty instead of half full. If your attitude is negative, then you see cooperation as sucking up. You see being responsive to the boss' direction as sucking up to the boss. You see being a team player as sucking up. You see anything related to helping the boss be successful as sucking up, kissing butt, or brownnosing. If you go through your career and life that way, you will never impress your boss to get a good evaluation from him/her. It will also negatively affect your love life.

### Don't Suck Up and Fail

If you don't want to be successful, don't suck up. If you don't want to get good assignments, don't suck up. If you don't want to get awards, rewards, and recognition, don't suck up. If you don't want to get promoted, don't suck up. If you don't want to receive raises and bonuses, don't suck up. If you don't want to receive any perks, don't suck up. But don't ever complain to anyone about not receiving anything good from the boss. Remember, *you get what you give.*

> ***You get what you give.***

### Change Definition of "Sucking Up"

Now, if we would change the definition of sucking up, kissing butt, and brownnosing to any of the following instead, life would be much better for all of us:

- Being responsive to your boss
- Being cooperative with your boss
- Being a team player
- Being friendly with others including your boss
- Reporting status to your boss
- Being respectful towards your boss
- Being thankful to your boss
- Smiling at the boss always and laughing with him/her at times
- Asking your boss questions and for help

- Speaking well of your boss to others
- Giving your boss compliments

## Reasons for Promoting You

Remember, there are two reasons why a boss hires you: (1) you can help him/her make money and (2) he/she likes you. Also, there are two reasons why a boss will promote you: (1) you can help the company make money and grow and (2) he/she likes you. Your skills, ability, and hard work will get you to achieve #1. However, if you don't do all of the things in the above bullet list, you will not achieve #2. Doing #1 and #2 will get you promoted way before just accomplishing #1 or just #2. However, #2 only will definitely get you promoted much before #1 only. *You could be the hardest worker in the company, but if the boss dislikes you, forget about getting promoted.*

> *You could be the hardest worker in the company, but if the boss dislikes you, forget about getting promoted.*

## Networking and Relationships are Key

Until you learn this principle, you won't reap the fruits of your labor. If you are a good, hard worker, you are shooting yourself in the foot if you will not change your paradigm and do the things in the bulleted list above. Relationships are much more important than intelligence, knowledge, hard work, ability, talents, physical strength, good looks, and capability. This is why *networking is the most important tool for career success.* Successful networking means that you get along with people, have friends, work harmoniously with others, and mutually assist each other.

> *Networking is the most important tool for career success.*

## A Whole Different Perspective

You can go only so far with your sheer abilities. After that, other people must help you to achieve the top of the ladder or mountain. If you will not help others, others will definitely not help you. So, cast away the idea of sucking up. Replace it with befriending and working with your boss. It is a whole different perspective when you view things that way.

### Become an Insider

Usually, it is only the jealous ones who cannot cooperate with authority figures and who will badmouth anyone else who does cooperate with authority figures and, thereby, receive the promotions. Don't be on the outside looking in. Get in there and become one of the insiders. Change your paradigm today and become part of the power structure.

## Changing Companies to Get Promotions

*Do you think it will be faster and wiser to wait for getting promoted internally, or should I work for a few years and change to another employer, work at new employer for a few years to gain some new experience, and then come back to my first employer but in a higher-level position with higher pay? What is your advice on that?*

### A High-risk Approach

Your proposed strategy is a very high-risk approach that possesses a very low probability of success. If you just wait for a promotion internally, chances are, the promotion won't happen, and you'll be waiting forever.

### Make Things Happen

*To get promoted, you must make things happen.* You must work very hard and produce spectacular results that are recognized by everyone. You must network to get everyone thinking that you deserve to be promoted. You must let your supervisor know what your goals are and how she/he can help you in achieving those goals, which should include being promoted. If people aren't thinking about it, it won't happen.

> *To get promoted, you must make things happen.*

### Produce Results to Get Promoted

Working for a few years and then changing to another employer does nothing for you. You need to add value, be a mover and shaker, make things happen, and achieve things that create excellent bullets for your resume before you will be able to be promoted into a better job in another company.

## Accomplish Things to Get Promoted

Furthermore, just working at a new employer for a few years to gain some new experience does nothing for you. You must add value, be a shaker and mover, make things happen, and achieve things that create excellent bullets for your resume before you will ever be able to return to your first employer in a higher-level position with higher pay.

## Returning to a Previous Employer—Not a Good Idea

Additionally, returning to a previous employer is not a good thing to do unless they have searched you out and coaxed you to return to their company. If you initiate the move and they accept you, you are at a decided disadvantage. Things usually are not as good as they were before you left them. With all of the outstanding companies out there where you can work, it would be better for your career to go to a new company to advance your career.

## Find a New Company

If your original company is that good to return to, then why would you leave it in the first place? Usually, when you desire to leave a company, it is not that good of a company. So, why would you want to return after you worked at a better company? Find a new, even better company to work in. You will be happier and more successful in a new, better company than returning to a former company. *Expect the best and get it!*

> *Expect the best and get it!*

## *How to Cope With Being Promoted*

*I have worked with the same company for the last seven years and was recently promoted to management. My co-workers are some of my best friends, and it puts me in an awkward position when I have to tell them what to do. How would you recommend my getting over that awkward feeling?*

## Palsy-walsy No More

You must realize that when you are promoted into management, your relationship must change between you and your subordinates. When you were peers or co-workers, you were palsy-walsy. As a manager, you are not peers any longer. Therefore, you cannot be palsy-walsy any longer. Instead, you are now peers with other managers on the same level as you. So, you can be palsy with those other managers.

### Maintain a Supervisor-Direct Report Relationship

If you cannot separate friendship from a supervisor-direct report relationship, then you will have a difficult time managing your direct reports. If you cannot handle that difference, then you will not be able to be a good manager to your direct reports. You can be cordial, professional, friendly, and respectful of your former pals, but you cannot maintain your palsy-walsy relationship.

### Close Friendships on the Job

You can still be best friends with your former co-workers, but you must keep that close friendship off the job. You cannot display close friendship on the job because if your direct reports cannot separate being close friends and cannot properly receive directions, orders, or assignments from you, you will experience relationship problems on the job. Another drawback of close friendships on the job is that if you are not equally friendly with every direct report, some will accuse you of favoritism. You will lose either way.

### Get Used to It

So, I would say, get used to the awkward feeling. If you cannot get used to it, perhaps you should not remain in management and go back into the ranks and be palsy-walsy with your best-friends and co-workers. *You cannot have your cake and eat it too.*

> *You cannot have your cake and eat it too.*

## What to Consider in Accepting or Declining a Promotion

*I am currently in a situation where my company, Hollywood Video, offered me a promotion from a shift director to an assistant manager. This would require me to change locations to a store farther away, which just opened a couple of weeks ago. I've talked to every person who must approve the transfer request. I spoke with my store manager, my district manager, the store manager at the new store, and the district manager of the new store.*

*I have approval from everybody, but I do not believe they gave me a fair offer. The increase in pay, basically, covers my time and gas to travel to the new store. The job is, basically, the same but with more responsibility for the store. I do not believe I will take this opportunity. Is there anything else I should consider before accepting or declining the offer?*

### Considerations in Accepting or Declining an Offer

Everything we do depends on our values, motivation, and passion. From what you've already mentioned, you have made your decision to reject the promotion. Before accepting or declining this offer, you should consider the following items:

- ***Impact on Your Future with the Company.*** Will the decision to reject the promotion hurt you in the future with this company? If you're not going to make a career of this company, then it won't hurt you much. If you are making a career of the company, it may definitely hurt you. However, the degree of hurt is a function of the quality of your management.

- ***Does it Help Your Resume or Not.*** Will the promotion make my resume look better? Most definitely! It will create a bullet that packs a punch. Is that important to you?

- ***Perception.*** The promotion will definitely provide you with more experience, particularly for being responsible for the store. Even though you may feel that the job is basically the same as your current job, the perception of others, such as hiring managers, would be that the job was greater than your current job and contributed to your personal growth. That's just the perception generated, but *perception is everything*.

> ***Perception is everything.***

  - ***Basically the Same Job?***
    I hope you wouldn't go into an interview and tell the interviewer that even thought the title of assistant manager sounds much better than shift director, it was basically the same job. Do you get my drift? A hiring manager would automatically assume that the assistant manager's position required much more work and responsibility than a shift director's position…unless you convince him otherwise of course.

  - ***Perception of the Better Job Title***
    Hence, perception of the better job title works automatically in your favor. That's why many people seek the title of manager. Managing the flow of cars is much more important than directing traffic because you would have a bunch of traffic directors reporting to you. Do you get that?

- *Negotiation.* You stated, "I do not believe they gave me a fair offer." Was this the result after you aggressively negotiated with them for the best offer? On the other hand, did you just accept what they offered you? If you didn't negotiate, shame on you. *Everything is negotiable.*

> *Everything is negotiable.*

  o *Use Your Leverage*

   If you accepted this unfair offer, then that's all you're worth. So, if it is not a fair offer, counteroffer! You don't particularly want the promotion anyway. They want to promote you. Hence, you have all the leverage in the world to get a very good offer. You are in the driver's seat. You have nothing to lose but all to gain. So, why don't you use that leverage?

  o *Ask for the World*

   If you asked for the world and they withdrew the offer and promotion, so what! You didn't want the promotion in the first place. You lost nothing. But you put into their minds what you really believe you're worth. Do you understand what I am driving at here?

  o *Gain Good Experience Negotiating to the Hilt*

   Negotiate the offer to the limit. Here is an opportunity for you to gain good experience negotiating to the hilt because you're not afraid of them withdrawing the promotion and offer. Do you get my drift? Ask and you shall receive.

### Why You Consider Rejecting the Promotion

In a way, I can see why you are considering rejecting the promotion. On your Jung Typology Test (JTT) or Myers-Briggs Type Indicator (MBTI), you are an ENFJ (Extroverted feeling with intuiting), and you are highest on "J" judging. Furthermore, on your Career Success Map Questionnaire (CSMQ), you scored high on "Getting Free" and "Getting Balance." The promotion satisfies neither of these two orientations. You're not the "Getting Ahead" or the "Getting High" type, both orientations of which you scored lowest.

### Do What Makes You Happy

Whatever your decision, do what makes you happy. *There is nothing worse than working a job that's pure drudgery to you.* Since I believe your current passion is to become a financial

> *There is nothing worse than working a job that's pure drudgery to you.*

investor or financial analyst, you should seek employment that allows you to work with money, capital, or purchasing power. These preparatory jobs could be a cashier, teller, accountant, or anything else that allows you to handle and/or deal with money. Then, leverage those preparatory financial jobs that will lead you to becoming a financial investor or financial analyst. That's the path you should take.

## Would Declining a Promotion Be Detrimental to My Career?

*In my current position, a lot of my supervisors and fellow employees see me as someone who should be promoted fast. I am excited that people see me as having these qualities, but I don't see myself going for a promotion for another three years. How do you respectfully decline a promotion but still let management know you are interested but you want to build on your foundation before you just jump into something? I don't want to burn any bridges.*

### An Unusual Person

You are an unusual person. Most people would jump at the chance of a promotion, particularly an early promotion and assume the risk of failing. However, only you know yourself best. If you feel an early promotion would be detrimental to your performance and abilities, then you are probably correct and are wise to feel the way you do about delaying the promotion.

### The Management You Work for is Important

If you work for good management, they would not take your respectfully declining a promotion as an affront to them and hold it against you for all future promotions. On the other hand, if you work for lousy management, they would hold it against you and blackball you for future promotions just to punish you.

### Understand Your Management's Motivation

You need to understand thoroughly the motivation of your management to promote you early. If they think very highly of you and move you up way before your time, they would help you to be successful and would overlook some of your mistakes and shortfalls when you commit them in your new job. However, if they are just throwing you into the "deep end of the pool" and don't really care whether you sink or swim, you then may be in trouble.

## Work for Good Management

So, if you work for great management, you will be okay, but if you work for lousy management, then they will allow you to fail. *Good management who are grooming you for greatness will always help you to be successful.*

> *Good management who are grooming you for greatness will always help you to be successful.*

*Chapter 7*

# Negotiating Raises

---

*Be aware that when you attempt to negotiate a salary that is outside normal policy or timing, then you are attempting to control or at least influence the behavior of a very big and complex system, i.e., your organization. The more you can understand what this system needs, and how it operates in terms of making these decisions, including all the personal factors affecting managers and executives, then the better chance you have to achieve an improvement.*[19]

Alan Chapman

## Negotiating Raises and Higher Starting Salaries

*You say one should never accept the first "salary" offer when it comes to getting a job, but in your book, you also state, "if you lack experience, sometimes accepting the first offer is necessary." When do you know the time is right to be "negotiating" raises or higher starting salaries?*

### When You Have Leverage, You Can Negotiate Effectively

The right time to be "negotiating" raises or higher starting salaries is when you have **leverage**. *When you have leverage, you will know it.* You will feel it. You will have an ingrown confidence that you can do better. When the hiring company comes a courting, you

> **When you have leverage, you will know it.**

---

19 Alan Chapman, "salary negotiation tips: tips and techniques for salary negotiation for employees, and salary negotiation tips for managers," copyright by Alan Chapman 1995–2005, extracted from the free resources website http://www.businessballs.com on 6/28/05. Alan Chapman accepts no liability for any arising issues.

know you have leverage. When you have two or more simultaneous offers, you know you have leverage. When they throw benefits and other perks at you, you know you have leverage.

### When You Have Leverage, You Know It

I once had a direct report who had received an offer from another company. She was an outstanding worker. I wrote up an outstanding annual review on her. She had bachelor's and master's degrees. She had applied for a proposal administrator's job vacancy, but the company came back and offered her a proposal manager position instead. She knew she had leverage.

### When You Have Leverage, You Can Get What You Want

She was not happy with the initial base salary they had offered her. She negotiated and got the salary she wanted. She also got them to give her 3,300 shares of stock options! She had leverage. Do you now understand when someone has leverage? She can get what she wants in negotiating the best offer possible because she was in the driver's seat. That's the kind of leveraged position you need to be in.

## How to Get a Raise

*Let's say I got a job at an entry level marketing position and had it for about two years. The company is great, but I want to get paid more. Should I just quit now and get a job somewhere else or stay within the company and ask for a raise?*

### Make a List of Your 10 Significant Accomplishments

In a two-year time period, you should have accomplished great and wonderful things for the company. If you cannot make a list of 10 significant things (not required in your job description) you have achieved to move the company forward, forget about asking for a raise. If you have accomplished at least 10 fantastic projects, you should have automatically received at least two raises by the time two years went by. If you have done great things and haven't yet received a raise, get out of there and go work for a better company.

### It is Obvious When One Deserves a Raise

However, what usually is the case is that most employees just do a passable job and they expect the world from the company. That will not fly! If you are not looked up to by your peers, you probably do not deserve a raise. If your peers do not automatically assume you should get a raise because of your performance and results, then you do not deserve one. When someone deserves a raise, it is obvious because of his/her great achievements, and everyone knows it.

### Get of Your Fat Duff and Do Something

People who do very little but expect the world can find another job at another company. However, if they keep doing the same average job as they did in the previous company, they won't get a raise there either. So, the thing that they really need to do is to get off their fat duffs and discover something, create/invent something, innovate something, and/or bring in huge sums of revenue into the company. When they do that, then and only then do they deserve a raise.

## How to Ask for a Raise

*What is the most appropriate way to ask for a raise? How do you go about asking for a raise?*

### Ask for a Raise Face-to-Face

The most appropriate way to ask for a raise is to go into your supervisor's office, sit down, and face-to-face ask him/her for a raise. The worse he/she can do is to say "no." He/she won't kill you. Asking eyeball-to-eyeball is more effective than sending him/her an email or calling by phone. When you ask face-to-face, you can watch your supervisor's eyes and body language. The answer will most likely be "no," but the eyes and body language will clue you in to determine if you will ever receive a raise.

### You Must Ask

Asking also instills in your supervisor's mind that he/she will probably need to seriously consider giving you a raise the next time it is possible, particularly if you are doing outstanding work. If you don't ask, your supervisor may think you are happy with the current situation. By asking, that makes your supervisor aware that you expect something for your good work. That's the key. *If you are not doing good work, forget about asking for a raise.* Only if you are doing superior work will you have the leverage to shake loose a raise in the near or distant future. So, ask and ye shall receive (only if you are doing good work as agreed to by both you and the person with the gold).

> *If you are not doing good work, forget about asking for a raise.*

## Be the Best Producing Direct Report

As I said before, there is no better way to ask for a raise than to point-blank ask your boss for that raise. However, you had better have a lot of leverage when you ask for that raise. In other words, you had better be the best producing direct report of all those that report to him/her. *If you are an average producer, forget about asking for a raise.* He/she would probably laugh you out of his/her office.

> *If you are an average producer, forget about asking for a raise.*

## Ask When Your Supervisor is in a Good Mood

The best time to ask for a raise is when your supervisor is in a good mood, say, because you were the primary person responsible for capturing a $10 million contract that day. When the moment is right, pop your supervisor the question. For example, you could say, "John, since I was instrumental in capturing this $10 million contract, would it be appropriate for me to receive a good raise to reward me for my efforts?" Then, look your supervisor straight in the eyes and wait for the answer. Do not say another word. Just wait for the answer.

## They Won't Turn You Down Flat

John will probably say, "I'll see what I can do." That's the best way to do it. Company management would be stupid to turn you down flat. If you are rejected immediately, start looking for a better company for which to work. Your management would be a bunch of losers to turn you down flat.

## In Lieu of a Raise

If they cannot give you a raise, they can give you something else to appease you. For example, they can give you any one or a combination of the following items in lieu of a raise:

- A nice bonus
- A top company award (large plaque)
- A vacation to a tropical location (like attending a week-long conference in Hawaii)
- Recognition in the company newspaper
- A nicer office

- Free dinner tickets
- Free tickets to the World Series or the Super Bowl Game
- A promotion to a better position
- Personal laptop computer
- BlackBerry phone

You can name many other things here. There is a whole host of things that the company can give you for the great job you did. So, "*ask and ye shall receive.*"

> **Ask and ye shall receive.**

## When to Ask for a Raise

*If an employee feels deserving of a raise, when would be a good time to confront his/her supervisor with this request?*

### Ask Only When Warranted

Asking for a raise is only warranted if an employee has good reasons for a raise, not just because he/she "feels deserving of a raise." For example, if the employee hasn't received a raise in two years and he/she has accomplished a lot of obviously good things for the company that everyone attributes to him/her, then and only then should he/she ask his/her supervisor for a raise.

### You Must Have Done Something Significant

If the employee hasn't done anything but come to work every day, work eight hours a day, and just did what was on the job description, he/she doesn't really deserve a raise. In that case, I personally wouldn't ask for a raise. The employee would be laughed at, scorned, and/or chased out of his/her supervisor's office.

### Examples of Significant Accomplishments

However, on the other hand, if the employee accomplished the following, he/she would have more of a case upon asking for a raise:

- Brought in a large percentage of the company's revenue for the past two years
- Traveled widely for the company

- Sacrificed greatly for the company by performing many hours of free overtime work
- Garnered the company some valuable recognition for a major newsworthy accomplishment
- Saved the company a significant, measurable amount of money
- Performed major projects successfully for the company and received numerous letters of praise from customers
- Discovered, created, invented, innovated, and/or achieved major developments for the company during the past two years
- Landed major contracts or closed major deals
- Led a major proposal effort as proposal manager that won millions of dollars of new business
- Helped the company double in size largely because of the employee's efforts
- Solved a major problem the company has been struggling with for years

## You Must Get Things Done

Do you get the picture? An employee must be "a mover and a shaker" in the company. He/she must "add value" to the company. He/she must "make a difference" in the company. He/she must be "a recognized go-getter" in the company. He/she must not only be well liked but one who "gets things done" in the company.

## When You Deserve a Raise

If an employee exemplifies all of these characteristics, he/she deserves a raise. Then, the employee has leverage, and when he/she asks for a raise, top management will listen and try to do something for him/her lest he/she voluntarily leaves the company for greener pastures.

## Raises are for Winners, Not Losers

So, if one comes to work late every day, do very little, complains a lot, takes long breaks, and just passes the time away, he/she should not dream of asking for a raise. Raises are only for those who build the company, not for those who drain the company of cash by just existing in spending jobs and collecting a paycheck.

## Most Employees Should Be Grateful They Have a Job

Unfortunately, everyone feels he/she deserves a raise all the time. This mindset is what makes life difficult for supervisors. However, if he/she does what is in the bulleted list above, then he/she can feel comfortable asking for a raise. If not, the employee should forget about it and be grateful he/she has a job!

*Chapter 8*

# Negotiating Your Own Position Title

---

*I just wanted to write you to say thanks for all of the valuable skills that you taught us in you last Career Development course! During the class, I thought it was all very valuable, but I didn't think that it was going to be this valuable!*

*During my job search, everything I did came straight from what you taught us through your class and through your book. I interviewed with four different companies and had great success with all interviews. I received two offers before I graduated!*

*Because of what I learned from you, I began to be more confident in myself and what I had to offer these companies. I eventually accepted a position with a company that "created a new position" for me!*

*This is my second week, and things are going great! So, anyways, I wanted to pat you on the back, and give you an update on my career search. Thanks again!*

Andrew Brockhaus
CSUSM Graduate

In your job search, work at creating a new position just for yourself. Also, work at increasing or elevating the position title for which you are applying. It can be done, and job seekers do it quite often. That is always part of my strategy whenever I apply for any advertised position vacancies. That should also be part of your overall job-searching strategy.

### Examples of Title Expansions

#### Proposal Specialist Expanded to Manager—Technical Proposals

You can create an unadvertised job in hiring companies. *Remember, advertised jobs are not the only jobs you can obtain.* Often you can create either a new, unadvertised job or improve the title of your job. For example, I once applied for a job with the title Proposal Specialist. Before I accepted the job, the job title was increased to Manager—Technical Proposals.

> **Remember, advertised jobs are not the only jobs you can obtain.**

#### Proposal Manager Expanded to Director of Business Development

I once applied for a Proposal Manager position with a company in Oklahoma City. By the time I had received an offer from that company, the position title had expanded to Director of Business Development. Not bad! *Remember, no advertised position title is cast in concrete.* If a company really wants you, they will change a title to make it more appealing to you.

> **Remember, no advertised position title is cast in concrete.**

#### General Manager Expanded to Vice President and General Manager

A time before, I had applied for a General Manager position. After receiving the job offer, I negotiated the title to a better-sounding Vice President and General Manager. Most of the time, it is no problem for the hiring executive to offer you a title more impressive than the advertised one particularly if you are negotiating with the CEO. So, always go into negotiations intending to improve your title.

### Propose New Ideas to Create Positions

#### Plan to Create a Division and Position

I once prepared a plan to establish a division of an East Coast company here on the West Coast. Since the company president was here on a business trip, I made an appointment to propose an idea to him. At least he was interested enough to meet with me. He took home my 30-page written plan to evaluate. Nothing came of it, but *"nothing ventured, nothing gained."*

So, any time you can come up with an idea that an executive would be interested in, try it. Who knows? Some day you might hit pay dirt and actually create a position for yourself. Like I said, *"nothing ventured, nothing gained."*

> ## Nothing ventured, nothing gained.

## Create Your Own Empires

You can create your own positions by starting your own firms. I have done that before. For example, I currently serve as general manager and principal consultant of Bob Uda and Associates (BU&A), proposal development, career counseling, and counterterrorism R&D specialists. Previously, I was president of BU&A. Furthermore, I am currently Owner of Buda Books Publishing, a book-writing and publishing company.

Previously, I had formed other companies. I served as Chairman, President, and CEO of Apollo Systems Technology, Inc. (AST), an R&D, engineering support services, proposal consulting, and manufacturers representative firm. I had also served as President of Systems Technology Services (STS was the predecessor of AST prior to its incorporation). Before that, I had served as President of Udaco, a publishing company.

## Working for Free to Create a Position

### Not a Bad Strategy

As mentioned previously in chapter 6, I have a good friend working on two ventures at no pay. He seeks venture capital for one and customers for the other. If he is successful on either one, he will have automatically created himself a new, paid position. He will then probably be able to formulate whatever title he wants in his new, full-time position. That is not a bad strategy to pursue.

### Creating My Own Positions

Personally, I have applied that strategy with two ventures with which I am associated. For example, I was appointed as Chairperson of the R&D Advisory Board of STARHUNTER Corporation of Maitland, Florida. Further, Dr. I. Stephen Tuba, president and CEO of the International Technology Foundation (ITF) recently appointed me as vice president as well as director of the "Technology in Economics Studies Program" (TiESP) of the International Technology Institute (ITI) of San Diego, California. We co-authored a book on *The Third Resource*. As can be seen, these are examples of what can be done to create one's own positions.

*Chapter 9*

# Negotiating Consulting Gigs

*One of the trickiest parts of being an independent contractor is negotiating payment and terms for a project. Overbid, and you may lose the job; underbid, and you won't receive what your services are worth. An extremely low bid can also cost you the contract if it makes the client think you don't know what you're doing.*[20]

Meredith Little
Freelance writer

Work at acquiring consulting contracts (both paid and free). Adding consulting assignments to your resume builds up your stature in the eyes of resume reviewers. It also helps you to acquire further consulting gigs.

## Negotiating Consulting Contracts

When you negotiate a consulting contract, make sure you cover all costs of benefits/perks within your proposed hourly rate. You should initially propose at least $100 per hour and work from there, but do not go below $75 per hour. These cheapskates will pay you $50 or less per hour if you will accept it.

You should be working for no less than $50 per hour base salary as a full-time employee. The benefits/perks (minimum of $25 per hour) should be on top of that. That is why I feel no consultant should accept less than $75 per hour. That

---

20 Meredith Little, "Creative Methods for Negotiating Contracts for Your Consulting Gigs," *TechRepublic.com*, published 2/17/00 at the following URL: http://techrepublic.com.com/5100-6333_11-1028262.html. Meredith Little is a technical writer, documentation specialist, trainer, business analyst, photographer, and travel writer.

is what those chintzy people at one company paid me for the three-months of consulting work I did for them. Fortunately, I was able to work a lot of overtime, so I made over $57K for those three months of contract work.

## Examples of Consulting Contracts

To give you an idea of consulting contracts that I have performed, I list the following contracts:

- Titan Systems Corporation (TSC) Communications Products Division (CPD) Prophet signals intelligence management system production program pursuit. Served as proposal administrator. Prepared overall work status sheets and kept track of work progress, 2002.

- Titan Systems Corporation (TSC) CPD Ka-band Satellite Augmentation Terminal (KaSAT) pursuit; assisted in winning the $22 million KaSAT contract. Served on the pink team review, prepared the executive summary, and significantly contributed to the performance risk and subcontractor management volumes, 2002.

- Tybrin Corporation's Edwards Air Force Base Operations on the Air Force Flight Test Center (AFFTC) Systems Engineering and Technical Assistance (SE/TA) contract; improved the program work breakdown structure for better visibility and cost collection, 1995.

- Hughes Aircraft Company (HAC) Radar and Communications Sector (El Segundo, California) on the Digital Airport Surveillance Radar (DASR) pursuit; prepared the overall program approach, integrated product team program organization structure, and integrated product and process development (IPPD) process flow strategy, 1995.

- Hughes Aircraft Company (HAC) Defense Systems Business Unit (El Segundo, California) on the CORPS Surface-to-Air Missile (SAM) pursuit; assisted in winning a $32M contract; prepared the design and development master plan, 1995.

- Hughes Aircraft Company (HAC) Defense Systems Business Unit on the Land Warrior (LW) pursuit; assisted in winning a $52M contract; developed the incremental integration testing and risk reduction evaluation strategy, program logic network, and combined master and summary milestone schedules, 1994.

- LB&M Associates (Lawton, Oklahoma), prepared a bibliography of physical security systems, 1987.

- General Connectors Corporation (Burbank, California); managed the Bell-Boeing V-22 Tilt-rotor proposal effort for compressed air ducts; prepared write-ups on design to cost (DTC), life cycle cost (LCC), and integrated logistics support (ILS); prepared reliability and maintainability program plans, 1986.

- Flight Systems, Inc. (Mojave, California); installed a configuration management system, 1986.

- General Dynamics Space Systems Division on the Peacekeeper Carry Hard Basing Program; prepared physical security system studies and analyses, 1986.

- General Dynamics Convair on the Tomahawk Cruise Missile Program; prepared an enhanced system security plan, 1986.

- General Dynamics Space Systems Division on the Medium Launch Vehicle Program; prepared the system security plan, ADP security plan, and operations security plan, 1986.

- General Dynamics Convair on the Small ICBM Program; prepared a system engineering management plan (SEMP), system requirements analysis (SRA) data and Type B3 specifications for missile handling equipment (MHE), MHE final report inputs, CDRL estimates, and human factors engineering (HFE) data, 1984–85.

- General Dynamics Convair on the Hard Mobile Launcher Program; performed risk assessment and analysis, 1984.

- Sears Machine Company; received retainer fee; performed manufacturer's representative services to sell machining of precision-machined parts, 1984.

- Tavco, Inc.; received retainer fee; performed manufacturer's representative services to sell high-pressure pneumatic systems and components, 1983–84.

## Networking is Key to Acquiring Consulting Gigs

These gigs indicate that I did some serious consulting. It wasn't just a passing fancy. Networking is extremely important. I initially started consulting for Hughes through a good friend of mine, who was a program manager there. That first gig at Hughes grew into other subsequent consulting gigs, which resulted from networking that I had established while there.

Once before, as I was searching for work at a career center, I befriended a fellow who also was seeking work. He found a good job with a contractor at Edwards

Air Force Base, California. After I had completed my consulting assignments at Hughes, I called him, and he gave me a consulting contract with his company. I worked on a Systems Engineering and Technical Assistance (SE/TA) contract, which improved the program work breakdown structure (WBS) for better visibility and cost collection. That was a wonderful experience.

*Appendix A*
# Testimonials

---

*Recently a fellow employee had a dispute with a leasing company over a quoted final settlement for a traded in car. The verbal promise by the lease manager was ignored by the billing department. After much negotiation the employee offered to meet halfway between the lower quote and the higher billing, but didn't want any further problems.*

*By printing out the May 2003 article by Michael Dennis on endorsing checks marked paid in full, I was able to provide the employee with the solution. The check was held for two weeks, while several more phone calls were made, but in the end, the check with its restrictions was accepted as payment in full. Funny how a caveat to one side of a dispute can become the solution to the other! The employee later visited the website and was impressed with the wealth of information available not just to credit managers, but to his field in accounting as well. Good job, CMA and Michael![21]*

Jim Fox,
District Credit Manager,
PDM Steel, Stockton

Testimonials indicate what people think about something. Positive testimonials give an idea of the effectiveness that a course or teacher has had on students. The following testimonials are from former students of my previous "Career Development" classes:

---

21 James Fox, "Testimonial to the Power of CMA Articles," *CMA News*, CMA Business Credit Services (CMA), Volume 1, Issue 3, August 13, 2003.

## Success in Job Seeking Using Proven Principles

One of my star students in my "Career Development" class wrote the below letter to me. I include it as a testimonial that these job searching principles, strategies, and tactics work in capturing good jobs.

*Hi Bob,*

*I accepted an offer for a job last week. Monday was my first day, and things are going very well. I got a job at a high technology company. I am the office manager and have a huge office; it's great! I think it is the perfect job for me right now, and I am learning a lot. I do not think I would have found a job as fast or with as much pay as I received without taking your course.*

*During my job hunting and interviewing process, I read your book and emails like they were my bible. I followed every step during the interviewing process for this job and received an offer at the end of the third interview. During the last interview with the CEO, I was not quite sure if I was going to get the job even though the interview was going very well. So, at the end of the interview, I told him how much I wanted the job and how well my skill sets would match this position.*

> **I read your book and emails like they were my bible.**

*I also asked about other applicants that I were up against. I couldn't believe how much information I received! I followed what you said and, basically, talked my way into the job. At the end of interview, he excused himself and came back five minutes later to offer me the job. I told him I would need some time and then later on was able to negotiate my salary to $37,000.*

*I would never have known that I could negotiate or that I should expect a good salary right out of college. I had people telling me that you are suppose to make around $25,000 for a year or so before you are worth anything. Thank you soooo much for saving me from a lot of poverty. I am very grateful for your class and your speeches about expecting things in life. Thank you, thank you, thank you!!*

*A Graduate*

## Use a Career Coach for Salary Negotiations

Here is a letter from another star student who followed correct principles in job seeking.

*In early December of 2003, I set a goal to find a job before I graduated. During this time, I was actively writing and re-writing my resume numerous times. I also started to gather references and to network.*

*With these resources, I acquired several letters of recommendation to include in my portfolio. As my last semester of my undergraduate degree began, I heard about the Career Development course and decided to add that class to further help me in preparing for the job search.*

*During the first half of the course, I communicated heavily with Bob Uda and used his knowledge as a career coach to launch my career. After 2-½ months of searching, I landed a job as a pricing and financial analyst.*

*Along with career coaches, I asked experienced workers to assist me in the salary offer/counteroffer process. With their help, I was able to obtain a starting salary and a raise in 90 days if my performance so merits. I started working full time while completing my last semester.*

*BSBA Alumnus*

## Career Class Should Be a Requirement

Charles Santilena, one of my super-fine students, writes me the following letter telling of his successes.

*Dear Bob,*

*My name is Charles Santilena. I was in your Career Development class last semester. I learned so much in your class on interviewing, resume building, and negotiating salary. You were right [when you said that] you are only as good as what you accept and not to sell yourself short.*

*I recently went through the interview process and landed a great job. I went through four grueling interviews—one with the president/owner of the company. Each interviewer said that I did awesome and asked if I had a lot of interviewing experience. Your class prepared me extremely well for this.*

*I also negotiated my pay. I was originally offered a entry level position starting at $30K/year plus bonuses of about $2–$3K/year. After my 2nd interview, I did so well that they offered me to interview for a higher position with an increase in pay. The position salary was $33–$36K/year plus $5k bonus. I was so happy they gave me the opportunity to interview for this.*

*One of the toughest questions they asked me was, "Why do you deserve the upper limits of the salary without any experience." I told them what the average student* *graduating with my degree is expected to make and explained why I would be a great fit for the job. I ended up at $500 below the top dollar amount…with no experience!*

*Thanks, I highly recommend your class to anyone in the business program. It should be a requirement!*

> ***I highly recommend your class to anyone in the business program. It should be a requirement!***

*Thanks again, Bob.*

*Charles Santilena (Senior Account Manager)*

*P.S. Feel free to share this story with your classes if you wish.*

### The Importance of Networking

Another of my finest students, Sandy Parlin, writes the following:

*Hi Professor Uda,*

*How are you? Congratulations on your 9th book! I don't know if you remember me or not. I am your former student who had the dilemma of buying a condo a month before graduation and getting stuck with my cocktailing job. Well, it took me a little while but I've finally taken the much anticipated step of delving into a career.*

*I have recently signed on with Coldwell Banker as a realtor where I will work alongside my sister. I am still in the training phase (only 3 more weeks left), but I feel so much better that I have embarked on a career. One thing that I learned from you that has become very prevalent is the importance of networking and joining different committees or groups in the community.*

*Thanks for all the wisdom you passed on in your class. Again, congratulations on your new book…I look forward to reading it!*

*Sincerely, Sandra Parlin*

## The Importance of Branding

Chaz Brewer, a phenomenal success story, writes of his successes in the following letter:

*Dear Bob Uda:*

*I am excited to announce my recent achievement of receiving my Real Estate Salesperson's License and becoming a Realtor. On October 18th 2005, I was issued a license from the California Department of Real Estate. I am now ready to begin acting under the full capacity of my license.*

*I have been working as an assistant manager for Mortgage Funding from June 2004 until my promotion to manager in July 2005. During this period, I was and currently am engaged in the mortgage lending business. My position at Mortgage Funding has afforded me the opportunity to gain valuable experience and insight into the lending side of real estate. As an employee of Mortgage Funding, I have gained real estate transaction experience by selling foreclosed properties for the company.*

*I was born and raised in Santa Barbara. I am a graduate of California State University San Marcos. I hold a Bachelor of Science degree in Business Administration with an emphasis in service sector management. In addition, I am a member of the Santa Barbara Association of Realtors, California Association of Realtors, and the National Association of Realtors.*

*I sit on the Board of Directors for Mortgage Funding. I am active in the community by serving as the Financial Manager for the Santa Barbara Chapter of Christian Surfers United States. I have also earned a United States Department of Transportation Private Pilot's License.*

*If you or anyone you know are interested in buying, selling, or financing real estate I am here to serve you. I look forward to hearing from you in the near future.*

*Sincerely,*

*Charles Brewer*
*Manager/Realtor*

*P.S.—Thank you for sharing your ideas on "Brand You." This concept is very applicable to real estate sales and financing.*

### Doing What He is Passionate About

Phi Huynh, another of my super motivated, enthusiastic students, demonstrates that he is now doing his passion job.

*Hi Bob,*

*It is nice to see that many students have taken the importance of your course and, today, still apply it to their everyday living.*

*As for myself, I am currently a Learning and Sales Development Consultant for Wells Fargo Bank. My job, more or less, is to facilitate and teach the Culture, the Visions and Values, as well as job duties to all current and new team members who join the company with a focus of making each and every one of them successful on the job and in life. I facilitate anywhere from San Diego up to San Bernardino and the Inland Empire. I also support the Border States of Arizona and Texas.*

*A take away from all is this: I am doing what it is that I am passionate about. I have been given the opportunity to spread knowledge in the classroom in hopes of touching students' lives giving them a valuable lesson about the "Real World."*

> **I am doing what it is that I am passionate about.**

*Again, I would like to say thank you and hope all is well for you as well as to all the students.*

*Thanhphi Huynh*
*Wells Fargo Learning and Sales Development Western Region*

### The Importance of Interviewing Well

A wonderful former student sent this letter to me.

*I am sorry it has been so long since I talked to you. I had no idea that getting your career together would be SO busy! The last time I talked to you, I was in a crisis at my job and needed to get out. At that time, you did wonders for my resume.*

*When I was hiring for my position, the resumes that came in were ridiculous. I mean tripled space, three pages long when they could have been one page, and spelling errors! Thank you again for your class and your help.*

*After I quit my job, I worked on a marketing project for a few months at a commercial bank. Now I am working as a sales and marketing coordinator at a great company. I couldn't have gotten here without your help.*

*Each interview I went on, I was always up against competition. It was never just me they were picking from. There was always at least one or two other people. But I was the one who always won, and I believe it was from what I learned in your class. I always closed the deal in the interview, and that was with the skills I learned in your class.*

*My resume got me in the door, but the interviewing skills help me beat the competition and get the job! Thanks Bob. Next semester, I will speak to your class because your material is priceless! That is why you have your own "Bob Uda" folder in my email account. Talk to you soon....*

> **Your material is priceless!**

*Former Student*

### An Extremely Positive Experience in Her Education

Danielle Birdsall is one of my finest former students who is on her way to a successful career. She writes the following letter.

*Mr. Uda,*

*Wow, 2005 as flown by! It seems as though my days at CSU San Marcos were not too long ago. I must admit that I miss school a great deal. I do wish to continue my education as soon as the opportunity presents itself. I am actually considering studying for my master's degree abroad as I recently received European Citizenship!*

*I am also looking into a possible career change in the near future. Although I am learning a great deal at Wells Fargo Financial, I know that I do not see this as a long-term career. I am planning to move toward counseling or, oddly enough, teaching career development. Taking "Career Trek" was an extremely positive experience in my education:) Well, we'll see what the future brings....*

*I hope that work is going well for you and that the holiday season treats you well! Merry Christmas and Happy New Year!*

*Danielle L. Birdsall*

It was just five months later when Danielle made a career change and is now working as an enrollment counselor with a great university. She said that she was finally pursuing her dream career and was very excited about it. The best part about it is that her employer has offered her 100 percent paid tuition for her master's degree in counseling. You cannot get any better than that!

# About the Author

Robert T. "Bob" Uda was born and raised in Hawaii for 20 years. He is the third of seven children of Masao and Irene Kuualoha Uda (both deceased). In the 40 years since leaving Hawaii, he has lived in Oklahoma, Ohio, Florida, Connecticut, and California with short stints in Utah, Alabama, Massachusetts, Texas, and Washington.

Bob earned BS degrees in aerospace engineering from the University of Oklahoma and in general business from Regents College of the University of the State of New York (now called Excelsior College). He further earned an MS degree in astronautics from the Air Force Institute of Technology and an MBA degree from the University of La Verne located in La Verne, California. Furthermore, he received a diploma in The Executive Program in Management from the UCLA Graduate School of Management.

Bob currently serves as proposal center manager with BAE Systems. Prior to that, he served as professor of systems acquisition management at the Defense Acquisition University (DAU) where he taught program management. He serves as a member of the Board of Regents (BOR) of the Institute of Certified Professional Managers (ICPM). Furthermore, he serves as director and vice president of the International Technology Institute (ITI).

In the USAF, he served as officer career manager of the Space and Missile Systems Organization (SAMSO), now called Space and Missile Systems Center (SMC).

An award-winning writer, Bob has prepared over 40 publications including 11 books, six of them related to career development (including this book). One of these books is titled *Career Quest for Young Professionals: How to Maintain a Competitive Edge Over Your Peers*. A second book is titled *Career Quest for College Graduates: Developing a Successful Career by Leveraging Each of Your Jobs*. A third book is titled *Career Quest for College Students: Career Development for Those Who Plan to Have a Successful Career*. A fourth book is titled *Resumes That Pack a Punch! Creating Beefy Bullets That Grab, Hook, and Wow Hiring Managers into Calling You for an Interview*. Additionally, a fifth book is titled *What Hue is Your Bungee Cord? Job Searching Strategies for Those Over 40 Years of Age*.

He taught logistics management courses to graduate students as an adjunct faculty member of National University. As a career coach with Bob Uda and Associates, he taught undergraduate students in "Career Development" as an adjunct faculty lecturer at California State University San Marcos. He also taught "Writing and Publishing" as an instructor with the Cal State San Marcos Extended Studies Office.

He is a fellow in the British Interplanetary Society, associate fellow in the American Institute of Aeronautics and Astronautics, executive member of the Academy of Management, Certified Manager (CM) with the Institute of Certified Professional Managers, and a founding charter member of the Association of Proposal Management Professionals.

Internationally recognized in community service, he is listed in 46 Who's Who publications including *Who's Who in the World*, *Who's Who in America*, *Who's Who in California*, and *Who's Who in Science and Engineering*. He was the District 12 Write-up Winner as well as the State Write-up Winner in the California Jaycees.

Along with co-authors Dr. Istvan Tuba and Dr. Anthony Etele, Bob received a Certificate of Excellence as a finalist in the Best Published Non-fiction Books of 2005, Politics and Social Science category, with their book titled *The Third Resource: A Universal Ideology of Economics* at The 12th Annual San Diego Book Awards sponsored by the San Diego Book Awards Association, Inc., on May 20, 2006.

Bob and his wife, the former Karen Elizabeth Rowland of Circleville, Ohio, sired two sons, a daughter, and four grandchildren. You can contact Bob Uda by emailing him at bobuda@roadrunner.com.

# Index

work  5, 6, 8, 95, 99, 100, 101
Work Experience  54
working  8, 97, 99
world class  66
worst-case scenario  8
Worth  36, 48
writing  x

*You are worth exactly what you accept*  13, 36
*You are worth only what you accept*  36

*you are worth only what you accept*  2, 41
*you are worth what you accept*  48
*You cannot have your cake and eat it too*  82
*you get what you give*  78
you owe me  73
*You should never accept the first offer*  54

Zerby, Alton B.  64

978-0-595-40729-3
0-595-40729-3